Wilma George is a university lecturer at the Department of Zoology and a Fellow of Lady Margaret Hall, Oxford. She is an authority on desert adaptation and rodent distribution and has explored the deserts of Africa in search of the elusive gundi, a unique African rodent. She has also worked in the deserts of North Africa and Australia, and in the Malay Archipelago where Wallace had the idea that shook Darwin into publishing *The Origin of Species*. She works closely with the Mendel Museum in Czechoslovakia. She is married to the novelist George Crowther.

Wilma George has published several books: *Elementary Genetics* (1951/1965); *Animal Geography* (1962); *Biologist Philosopher: a Study of the Life and Writings of Alfred Russel Wallace* (1964); *Eating in Eight Languages* (1968); *Animals and Maps* (1969) and *Gregor Mendel and Heredity* (1975).

Modern Masters

Darwin

Wilma George

Fontana Paperbacks

First published by Fontana Paperbacks 1982

Set in Lasercomp Erhardt

Made and printed in Great Britain by
William Collins Sons & Co. Ltd, Glasgow

Contents

'True originality consists in trying to behave like everybody else without succeeding,'
Cocteau.

1. A Bolt from the Blue

'Innumerable well-observed facts were stored in the minds of naturalists ready to take their proper places,' Darwin 1876.

On 1 July 1858, Sir Charles Lyell – Professor of Geology at King's College, London – and Dr Joseph Hooker of the Royal Botanic Gardens, Kew, sponsored two important contributions at the Linnean Society in London: *'On the Tendency of Species to Form Varieties, and on the Perpetuation of Varieties and Species by Natural Means of Selection* by Charles Darwin Esq. and Alfred Wallace Esq.' The contributions were read by the Secretary because Darwin was at home in Kent and Wallace was 12,000 miles away in the Moluccas. No discussion took place either because – as the President wrote in his annual report – it was not one of those 'striking discoveries which at once revolutionize, so to speak, the department of science on which they bear' or because – as Hooker thought – 'the subject was too ominous'.

The general reading public of nineteenth-century England did not take the proceedings of the Linnean Society but the apparently unremarkable event of 1858 provided advance publicity for the book that everyone then knew Darwin was writing. 'Wallace's impetus', Thomas Henry Huxley wrote jubilantly to Hooker, 'seems to have set Darwin going in earnest' and expectation was 'rife as to the forthcoming book'.

On the Origin of Species by Means of Natural Selection by Charles Darwin was published on 24 November 1859 and its 1250 copies sold out on the day of publication. By January, a second edition was on the market and new editions, revised by the author, continued to appear until 1872 by which time 24,000 copies in six editions had been printed. It had been translated immediately into German and Dutch and, in 1862, a French edition appeared. By 1876, Darwin was able to report translations into every European language in spite of the fact that – as Darwin himself confided to Hooker – 'my gracious, it is tough reading.'

The initial success of the *Origin* can be attributed to its perfect adaptation to the environment at the particular time at which it appeared. The time was right, the ground had been prepared in innumerable ways.

Transmutation or development was not a new idea in 1859. It had been creeping into the scientific world since the previous century when, for almost the first time, the Aristotelian outlook was challenged. The inorganic and organic worlds were being scrutinized by philosophers stimulated by all the new facts that were pouring in. Telescopes were pushing back the edges of the universe, naturalists were encircling the earth and miscroscopes were discovering life in a drop of water.

In Germany, Immanuel Kant had put forward a theory of cosmic evolution in his *Allgemeine Naturgeschichte und Theorie des Himmels* published in Frankfurt in 1755. The whole apparatus of the universe, he argued, had been brought into being by physical forces acting on raw matter according to discoverable mechanical laws. He considered the possibility of applying a similar theory to the organic world but recoiled because it was so 'incomprehensible to us that we feel ourselves compelled to conceive for it a different principle.'

At about the same time, the Comte de Buffon was questioning the age and structure of the earth. His conclusion that the earth was very old and had been formed gradually was, however, quickly suppressed by the Church and he was forced to recant: 'I abandon everything in my book respecting the formation of the earth, and generally all which may be contrary to the narrative of Moses.' The story of a changing earth was removed from the great *Histoire Naturelle* (1749–58) but, within its pages, lay subtle comments about the uselessness of the rudimentary toes in a pig's foot. No one, Buffon reasoned, would create a foot like that: therefore, the pig might have had an ancestor with four toes firmly planted on the ground. And he wondered that the tropics of South America and Africa – alike in climate – should have such different animals. Buffon's work was widely read: it was the standard work in biology for the eighteenth and nineteenth centuries.

Practical measures, too, were under way to test immutability and creation. In St Petersburg, in 1766, Joseph Kölreuter crossed varieties – or, as he thought, species – of the tobacco plant to find out whether he could make a new species from the cross. Hybrids from the cross were intermediate in character between the two parent plants. But, unfortunately, the pollen was sterile. He had not made a new species that could perpetuate itself but he had tried and, in trying, had initiated a long line of plant hybridization experiments. The fixity of the species, the stability of the natural world, was being questioned by experiment. By 1834, the University of Munich was offering a prize for a thesis on 'the causes of the mutability of species': which was won by Carl Gärtner, in whose father's garden Kölreuter had continued his St Petersburg experiments.

Around 1770, a society was formed in Birmingham. It attracted men of science like James Watt, Matthew Boulton, Josiah Wedgwood, Joseph Priestly and Charles Darwin's grandfather, Erasmus Darwin. The Lunar Society met informally to discuss the scientific problems of the day – like the nature of air and the pattern of the organic world – and provocative theories from at home and abroad: Buffon and that other Frenchman, Jean Baptiste Pierre Antoine de Monet de Lamarck; and the Scottish geologist James Hutton. Scientists were describing a changing world and the 'Lunatics' were at the centre of it. Priestly was looking for 'the great final cause': particularly 'in that part of philosophy which respects animal creation'. Lamarck had reclassified the animal kingdom for the first time since Aristotle and reclassified it according to natural affinities and arranged all organic beings in a branching relationship without gaps. Erasmus Darwin became convinced that animals changed shape and turned into new species – change had been brought about by the transmission of characters acquired during the lifetime of an individual – and all life, ultimately, came from the sea.

> Organic life beneath the shoreless waves
> Was born, and nurs'd in ocean's pearly caves;
> First forms minute, unseen by spheric glass,
> Move on the mud, or pierce the watery mass;
> These, as successive generations bloom,
> New powers acquire, and larger limbs assume;
> Whence countless groups of vegetation spring,
> And breathing realms of fin, and feet, and wing.
> (*The Temple of Nature*, 1803)

The transmission of acquired characters was an age-old theory but it had not been used to explain transmutation of species by natural means. Erasmus Darwin and Jean Baptiste de Lamarck were causing a stir in philosophical circles. In 1809, Lamarck had finally come out with *Philosophie Zoologique* in which he stated, categorically, that he believed that all living things had been developed, by natural causes, from other living things. Instead of taking the major groups of animals by leaps and bounds up the Aristotelian ladder, Lamarck transformed species from one to another by branching gently like a tree. Buffon was his text and Lamarck – no doubt – wondered about those pig's feet: why some birds had long legs, others had short; why some had claws, others had webs; why some had straight beaks, others had curved. In each case, it was clear to Lamarck that – during a lifetime – a bird strove to achieve something: there were birds that wanted to be waders and birds that wanted to eat nuts. So waders did their best to stretch their legs to walk into deeper water and nutcrackers did their best to crack bigger and harder nuts. The legs lengthened and the beaks strengthened as the birds strove harder and harder to achieve their goals; and some part of their achievement circulated in the blood stream until it reached the reproductive cells to be passed on to the offspring. Lamarck believed in organic continuity – *série* – and he had put forward a theory to account for it.

At the turn of the century, influential naturalists were querying the order of things; and finding support in the fast-growing science of geology.

Economic development in England needed practical geologists to advise on the siting of canals, the cutting of railways. Cutting into the earth exposed strange things: 'thunderbolts' – fossil molluscs – and fossils that had an uncanny likeness to sea urchins and corals. And the rock was layered, layer upon layer – and layered in different colours and textures. Some rocks would support railways and some hold water. It was essential to know how and where the rocks lay. Were the layers always in the same order? Were the layers the same in different parts of the country? As a result of systematic study of stratification – by arranging strata in a distinct and predictable order – a geological map of England and Wales was drawn in 1815 by William Smith. It was a revelation: some layers low down in Smith's sequence were exposed in some places; other layers, in other places; some layers were folded, some layers were tilted and some layers were turned upside down. Practical geologists were making discoveries about the earth's structure that would have unforeseen theoretical consequences.

Practical science stimulated theoretical science and – with the publication between 1830 and 1833 of Charles Lyell's *Principles of Geology* – theoretical geology entered a new phase in its history. Lyell's lesson was uniformitarianism based on Hutton's geology of an ancient earth with 'no vestige of a beginning – no prospect of an end'. Hutton believed transformations had occurred through heating of the rocks and his rivals attributed change to flooding. The earth, according to Lyell, had been shaped by the same processes that were still shaping it: earthquakes, floods, volcanoes and rivers; tipping and tilting, explosions and subsidence, erosion by wind and water. The earth was not stable and the earth – as Hutton found – was old.

By the 1830s, there was an uncomfortable feeling of change in the air and an uncomfortable feeling of living in one short moment of a vast extent of time. The universe changed according to mechanical laws, the earth changed through the operation of natural forces – animals and plants might change – and society was changing through political, economic and religious forces.

When *The Vestiges of the Natural History of Creation* was published anonymously in London in 1844 it brought together all those changing systems – universe, earth, plants, animals and man – into one developing whole. Everything went through stages and even the grades of mind were 'mere stages of development'. The *Vestiges* caused a stir. It came in for heavy criticism from professional scientists. The author was clearly no scientist: he was an easy victim for ridicule and vicious attacks. Huxley wrote a biting review; and Adam Sedgwick, Professor of Geology at Cambridge, picked it apart, found the details loathsome and finally decided that the book was so inept that it could only have been written by a woman. John Herschel, astronomer and philosopher, criticized the physics and Hugh Miller, amateur geologist, rejected the gradualism of the *Vestiges*. Miller claimed that geology did not provide evidence for gradual change from simple to complex. In *Footprints of the Creator or the Asterolepis of Stromness* (1847) he showed that complex fossils appeared suddenly in the rocks without predecessors. Thus, he argued, the evidence used in the *Vestiges* disproved gradualism and, therefore, also disproved evolution. The poor science of the *Vestiges* was easy to dismiss but it was not the real cause of the disquiet it had created. The real cause was dislike of a theory of change and a theory of change which had the temerity to include man.

But the *Vestiges* went through four editions in the first six months and was discussed and satirized by scientist and artist alike. Lady Constance – in Disraeli's novel *Tancred* of 1847 – recommended the hero to read a startling new book called *The Revelations of Chaos*. 'You know, all is development. The principle is perpetually going on. First there was nothing, then there was something; then, I forget the next, I think there were shells, then fishes; then we came. Let me see, did we come next? Never mind that; we came last. And the next stage will be something very superior to us; something with wings. Ah! that's it: we were fishes, and I believe we shall be crows. But you must read it.'

Darwin and Wallace both read the *Vestiges*; and, although Darwin professed not to be amused by it, he admitted that it was well written, had been more talked about than any recent work and had actually been attributed to him. Wallace thought it an 'ingenious hypothesis'. And the Reverend Baden Powell, Savilian Professor of Geometry at Oxford, wrote to the author congratulating him in the warmest terms.

The *Vestiges* was followed by Herbert Spencer's article in the *Leader* entitled 'The Development Hypothesis' (1850) in which he argued forcibly in favour of a doctrine of evolution. He assembled facts from geology and the new studies in embryology that were being pursued by Heinrich Pander and Karl Ernst von Baer in Germany and he concluded that the facts were there to substantiate a theory of organic change. Facts, perhaps, but not facts enough, cried the critics. 'Your own theory is supported by no facts at all,' retorted Spencer. Battle lines were being drawn up. Society was ready for the work that would heap fact upon fact and compel attention.

Darwin had been preparing a book – provisionally called *Natural Selection* – for years. It is difficult to be precise about how long because Darwin always worked on several projects at the same time. If an idea did not work he looked for another. He went over some old notes or tried some experiments. Always, however, jotting down the odd thought on the main theme.

Then, one fateful day – 18 June 1858 – Darwin received an article from the Malay Archipelago. Darwin was at his house in Kent, Wallace was in his hut in the Moluccas. Both men had been thinking about the 'species problem'. Darwin had made comments in his notebooks from 1839 onwards. Wallace had commented on the problem to his friend Henry Bates eleven years before sending Darwin his article 'On the Tendency of Varieties to Depart Indefinitely from the Original Type'. But when Darwin received that article from the Moluccas – which described in a few words what Darwin proposed to discuss in ten volumes – it was like a 'bolt from the blue'.

Wallace had committed to paper his thoughts on the transmutation of species in February 1855 while he was staying in Sarawak. 'On the Law which has Regulated the Introduction of New Species' argued that species had been formed from other species in branching lines. It drew on evidence from animal distribution, geology, classification and rudimentary organs. The article was published in the *Annals and Magazine of Natural History* in September 1855 but it received little attention. Wallace's agent informed him that several naturalists deplored his theorizing and it was two years before Wallace received an encouraging comment: from Bates – far away on the Amazon – and from Darwin. Darwin – in his first letter to Wallace – wrote that he agreed to the truth of almost every word of the paper and said he had himself been thinking along the same lines. But he did not tell Wallace that he had written, but not published, a 230-page essay on the subject in 1844.

It was obvious to Wallace that Darwin – and probably only Darwin – would be interested in the 1858 paper. Wallace was excited because he knew he had solved the problem of how new species could change: how the evolution, that some people were already coming to accept, could have been brought about. Darwin was shattered. There was nothing for it but to admit that he had been forestalled; or, perhaps, find a compromise. He consulted Lyell and Hooker who had heard of Darwin's work on species and knew that Wallace had given warning of his thoughts in 1855. Thus, part of Darwin's manuscript and a letter written to the American botanist Asa Gray in September 1857 were hastily prepared for presentation – with Wallace's 1858 paper – to the Linnean Society.

'How extremely stupid not to have thought of that,' exclaimed Huxley in London; but, at the Dublin Geological Society, the Reverend Samuel Haughton thundered that 'if it means what it says it is a truism, if it means anything more, it is contrary to fact.'

The 'truism' maintained that 'it can be shown' that there is 'an unerring power at work in *Natural Selection* (the title of my book), which selects exclusively for the good of each organic being' (Darwin) and that 'the life of wild animals is a struggle for existence . . . now let some alteration of physical conditions occur in the district . . . the superior variety would then alone remain . . . here, then, we have progression and continued divergence' (Wallace).

The theory was out and the stunning evidence followed. The *Origin* caused an uproar. But what was all the fuss about? It was fifteen years since the *Vestiges*.

Unlike the author of the *Vestiges*, Darwin was a scientist with years of experience in geology, botany and zoology and with all the fieldwork from the *Beagle* voyage to draw on. Darwin was impeccably accurate and he had assembled nearly 500 pages of facts. He was going to steamroller his audience into accepting his theory. His facts were to show not only that organic evolution had occurred but how it had occurred: by the mechanism that had been outlined in the 1858 papers, natural selection. Natural population numbers remained more or less constant: more offspring were produced than were required for maintaining the population; offspring differed from one another; only those that were adapted to the environment survived to reproduce the next generation; and if the environment changed it selected different survivors. The mechanism depended on the differential between the number of offspring produced and the number of offspring that survived. Picking up the argument from Robert Malthus's *Principle of Population* (1798) – which he had read for the second time in 1838 and which Wallace had read in the public library in Leicester in 1844 – Darwin wrote in the 1844 essay that, while food supply for species remained constant, organisms tended to increase in geometrical progression. In the *Origin*, he supported his statement with examples of the fly that laid hundreds of eggs, the tree that produced thousands of seeds; and a pair of elephants which, he calculated, would, if unchecked, provide the world with fifteen million descendants in 500 years. Apart from the human race, animals did not seem to be overpopulating the world. The flies' eggs were eaten or otherwise destroyed, most seeds failed to germinate and even the elephant's child was subject to catastrophe. Selection was the environment: the climate, the soil, the food supply and the predator. It eliminated the least adapted individuals. Conspicuous grouse were selected by birds of prey; and purple plums succumbed to disease more than yellow plums. There was no plan in the process of selection, no ultimate aim. A feature might be favoured in one set of conditions but selected against in another.

If selection were to operate there must not only be excess to select from but also variation. Darwin assembled an array of facts from dog breeders, pigeon fanciers and farmers. Variation among domestic animals and selective breeding for desirable characteristics provided Darwin with the perfect analogy for the variation and selection that occurred in the natural world. Selective breeding had been in full swing in England for many years. Land enclosure and the development of root crops made it possible to isolate animals and keep them over winter. Farmers established breeding programmes. By 1765, Robert Bakewell had set up breeding experiments for the improvement of sheep and cattle. Bakewell succeeded in establishing – by inbreeding and progeny testing – Leicestershire sheep and Longhorn cattle. By the nineteenth century, England was providing new breeds of cattle and sheep for the rest of the world. Darwin came from a country town and Wallace had surveyed land for enclosure. Both could appreciate Bakewell's achievements. Darwin drew attention in the *Origin* to Bakewell and other animal breeders for the care they gave to character assessment of the animal before selecting it for breeding. The racehorse and the pointer and, above all, the endless variety of pigeons were the results. Such examples were famous: dogs and pigeons, cattle and sheep. It made good argument by analogy for natural selection. It would have to be a subtle argument from the opposition to convince people that individuals did not differ when those differences could be selected for.

It was monumental and it was difficult to find fault with the detail. Darwin had been thinking about the subject for years and carefully collecting his facts. The *Origin* provided the scientific world with formidable evidence in favour of variation and selection as the explanation – based on Lyellian uniformitarian principles – of fossils, geographical distribution, rudimentary organs, embryological likenesses and classification.

The Darwin–Wallace theory was the first to provide a satisfactory mechanism for evolution. It was to the biological sciences what the Copernican revolution was to the cosmological sciences: a working hypothesis stimulating experiment and observation, a hypothesis whose repercussions were felt throughout society because the world would never look the same again. Just as the earth had been removed from the centre of the universe so man had been removed from the centre of life.

It 'provided us', Huxley wrote, 'with the working hypothesis we sought.' It has provided biological research with a working hypothesis for 123 years.

2. Time and Place

'The fact of the fossil remains of each formation being in some degree intermediate in character between the fossils in the formation above and below, is simply explained by their intermediate position in the chain of descent,' Darwin 1859.

Charles Robert Darwin was born in Shrewsbury on 12 February 1809, the son of a well-known and well-connected doctor. He spent seven years at Dr Butler's boarding school in Shrewsbury with little academic success and went on to study medicine at Edinburgh University. Disgusted by the medical course, he moved to Christ's College, Cambridge, where he prepared for an ordinary arts degree. But hunting, shooting and collecting were more to his taste than Euclid and philosophy. He collected beetles and he collected plants. He became friendly with John Henslow, the Professor of Botany; and he attended his classes and field trips so assiduously that he became known as 'the man who walks with Henslow'. Dr Darwin thought his son spent all his time on 'shooting, dogs and rat-catching' but he also read books – books which were to have a profound effect on his later thinking. The examination textbook, William Paley's *Evidences of Christianity*, prepared him for his later arguments against the widely-held belief in a designed universe and a designer. He read John Herschel's *Preliminary Discourse on the Study of Natural Philosophy* and was encouraged by the advice to the amateur to take an interest in natural science. He read *Personal Narrative of Travels to the Equinoctial Regions of the New Continent* by Alexander Humboldt – 'the greatest scientific traveller who ever lived' – who inspired him with an urgent desire to travel. But Darwin was by now destined for the Church – for a life 'blessed', as Herschel said, 'with an abundance of leisure'.

Darwin graduated in 1831 and immediately went on a

geological excursion to North Wales with Professor Sedgwick. At the end of August, he received a letter from the Professor of Astronomy at Cambridge telling him that he had been proposed as naturalist on a scientific expedition to Tierra del Fuego. A letter from Henslow gave more detail; for it was Henslow who, unable to go himself, had proposed Darwin. There was no pay and no official appointment attached to the proposal and Dr Darwin was against it: he saw it as yet another waste of time, yet another failure of his son to settle down to a profession. However, a successful appeal to uncle Josiah Wedgwood to plead his cause changed Darwin's life. On 27 December 1831, Charles Darwin left Plymouth in *HMS Beagle* with – among other things – a copy of the first volume of Lyell's *Principles of Geology*.

Between 1832 and 1836, the *Beagle* sailed up and down the coast of South America, charting the waters: sailing to the Galapagos Archipelago and across the Pacific to New Zealand and Australia, sailing round the Cape of Good Hope and touching South America, before sailing for home. This was the great adventure – Darwin's only experience of distant lands. At the beginning of 1839, he married his cousin Emma Wedgwood and settled in London but, after the birth of his second child, the family moved to Down in Kent, a two-hour journey from London. Untroubled by financial problems but frequently suffering from ill-health, Darwin lived at Down until his death on 19 April 1882.

On returning from the *Beagle* voyage, Darwin had a pile of notebooks and was required to write up the scientific achievements of the voyage. He sorted his specimens, prepared his journal for publication and, in July 1837, opened his first notebook on the species question.

The *Journal and Remarks 1832–36* (1839) contained day-to-day descriptions of the natural history of the *Beagle* voyage round the world under Captain James FitzRoy. Darwin wrote the geology for the official report but his zoological collections were described by experts: Richard Owen, George Waterhouse,

Leonard Jenyns, John Gould and Thomas Bell (who was to be President of the Linnean Society when the Darwin–Wallace papers were read in July 1858). Hooker described the botany of the Galapagos Islands but most of Darwin's carefully-collected plants – which he had sent to Henslow – were never described.

Darwin regarded himself as a geologist and his first scientific articles were geological. The first entry in his first notebook in 1832 was a description of that 'miserable spot', one of the volcanic Cape Verde Islands. He and Captain FitzRoy walked the islands, as Darwin had walked before with Henslow, FitzRoy taking measurements to determine the exact position of the islands and Darwin looking with fascination at the layering of the rocks. Darwin was surprised: the layered rocks of the Cape Verde Islands did not conform to his preconceived ideas – preconceived on the basis of his three-week training in geology with Sedgwick. But Darwin was a good observer and an honest observer, so he wrote in his notebook: 'although this old sea coast is 30 to 40 feet above the present level of ocean yet in others the present breccia again covers it, owing to having sunk again most likely . . . what confusion for the geologist.' Confusing for a catastrophist geologist like Henslow or Sedgwick – for a vulcanist, for a neptunist – but less confusing for a young man with a copy of Lyell's *Principles* in his cabin. Darwin had been warned by Henslow on no account to accept Lyell's views but already the geology of Saint Jago in the Cape Verde Islands was making Darwin suspicious. By the time he published *Geological Observations on the Volcanic Islands, Visited during the Voyage of HMS 'Beagle'* (1844) he was a converted Lyellian. Uniformitarianism – gradual change – was the explanation of the formation of the earth.

Catastrophism, however, was still the current theory. Sedgwick and Henslow were both catastrophists though not, perhaps, in the exaggerated sense in which Georges Cuvier had expounded it. Even if there had not been wholesale destruction and re-creation of the world – on the Cuvierian model – there might have been local catastrophic floodings, extinctions and re-creations. Darwin's first thoughts on South American geology were conventionally catastrophist. South American 'diluvial' deposits were evidence of a vast flood: it could be seen on the coast of Argentina, 'covered by diluvium and sand hillocks'.

Eventually, Lyell was victorious: by the time Darwin left South America, he was a convinced uniformitarian geologist, convinced that the continent of South America was slowly rising, moulded by erosion, volcano and earthquake. Fossil shells on the tops of mountains – similar to living forms on the beach below – were evidence of past elevation. An earthquake, experienced in Chile, had raised the ground several feet; and provided Darwin with what he considered spectacular evidence that elevation was still going on. The earth was in flux, changing as it always had done. Parts of the land had been covered by sea, parts had been elevated. Land had sunk, had twisted, had been eroded by water and wind – just as Lyell described.

But was not Lyell wrong about coral reefs? Darwin was no slave to Sedgwick's authority, so why should he be a slave to Lyell's? The reefs and atolls so plentiful in the Indian Ocean were very different from the coral formations of the West Indies. 'The subject of coral formation has for the last half year been a point of particular interest to me. I hope to be able to put some of the facts in a more simple and connected point of view than that in which they have hitherto been considered. The idea [Lyell's] of a lagoon island 30 miles in diameter being based on a submarine crater of equal dimensions', he wrote from Mauritius to his sister Caroline on 29 April 1836, 'has always appeared to me a monstrous hypothesis.' The entry in his notebook at the time – 'corals very different out and inside reef. Perhaps whole reef elevated' – showed his thoughts were running in other directions.

In 1842, *The Structure and Distribution of Coral Reefs, being the First Part of the Geology of the Voyage of the 'Beagle'* revolutionized coral reef studies. Building on the theory of Chamisso – who, having observed that corals grew more abundantly on the seaward side of the rock, suggested that it was an adequate explanation of reefs and atolls – Darwin argued that something more was required to account for the existence of old coral formations well below the level at which corals could grow. But first he needed confirmation of how corals grew. He spent several days exploring reefs and lagoons on Keeling Island in the Indian Ocean and found confirmatory evidence of abundant coral growth on the seaward side of reefs. Where there was mud and debris, inside the reef, corals did not grow. He had also noticed that coral growth was inhibited where muddy rivers ran off the land and caused gaps in the reef.

Chamisso was right about growth on the seaward side. The next step was to confirm reports that corals could only grow above 30 fathoms (55 metres). He and FitzRoy devised an experiment to test the depth hypothesis. They made soundings with a lead, capped with tallow; and they found that coral scratches became scarce below 20 fathoms and ceased at 30 fathoms. Corals, therefore, seemed to grow on the seaward side – where there was no mud and within the 30-fathom zone – further, corals could not tolerate exposure to air.

But it was impossible to believe that there were stationary platforms – all over the world, at exactly 30 fathoms – waiting to be colonized by corals. Anyway, even if coral growth and platforms were the explanation of some reefs, how could they account for all the different types of reef: fringing reefs, great barrier reefs and horse-shoe atolls? Darwin was convinced that coral barrier reefs and atolls went deeper than 30 fathoms. Below 30 fathoms, the coral was dead but once it had been alive. Neither Lyell nor Chamisso had offered an explanation that satisfied Darwin. Something more was needed.

That something might be land movement.

Darwin believed that volcanic activity was associated with land elevation. Were coral reefs and atolls related to volcanic activity? Darwin made a map of reef distribution and superimposed it on a map of volcanoes. In volcanic regions there were only fringing reefs. Thus, his map trick provided circumstantial evidence for a theory of fringing reef formation: volcanically elevated land with coral growth round the edges where light and temperature were appropriate.

Darwin's world map showed that barrier reefs and atolls – in marked contrast to fringing reefs – were not associated with volcanically active regions. Barrier reefs and atolls, therefore, might be formed on fringing reefs when the land stopped rising and started to subside. If the upward and outward growth of coral kept pace with the sinking land the fringing reef would be gradually transformed into one of the others. That land did sink was confirmed by the visible evidence of submerged cocoanut palms.

From a small fringing reef on an elevated island, to a barrier reef on a sinking island and, finally, to an atoll – as the island sank below the sea – was a logical sequence of events on Darwin's theory. With tilting, the occurrence of different reefs on opposite sides of an island could be brought into the theory. By cunning use of subsidence and elevation – and steady growth of reef-building corals – Darwin explained all reefs and atolls. It showed that Lyell had been wrong but it was based on strict Lyellian principles and Lyell accepted the new hypothesis immediately.

Darwin's publications during the fifteen years after his return to England and before the publication of the *Origin* were almost all geological. He had contributed fifteen papers on geological subjects and had written two books. He was welcomed as a geologist and attended meetings of the Geological Society of which he had become a member in 1836 and Secretary in 1837. Not all his contributions were as successful as *Coral Reefs*, still a standard work. An interpretation of the 'parallel roads' of Glen Roy on similar principles – slow rise above sea level – became unacceptable when Louis Agassiz reinterpreted the phenomenon to accord with his recent glaciation theory. Darwin was always annoyed that he had not made good use of glaciation theory.

Land movement was not the only interesting phenomenon to

emerge from the *Beagle* voyage. Fossils in South America had been a revelation. An expedition inland south of Montevideo in September 1832 had discovered fossilized remains of animals which Darwin guessed must have been of 'great dimensions'. He was delighted with his monster fossils and wrote enthusiastically to his sister Caroline about his wonderful luck in finding them. Eighteen months later, when he found a fossil mastodon in Patagonia, he wrote to his other sister, Catherine: 'There is nothing like Geology; the pleasure of the first day's partridge shooting or first day's hunting cannot be compared to finding a fine group of fossil bones which tell their story of former times with almost living tongue.'

What were those fossils? Were they evidence of previous creations, as Cuvier believed? Evidence that the world had once been populated by plants and animals which had been eliminated by floods, fires and earthquakes? Evidence that total new creations had been needed to start life again? The answer depended on several factors: whether the fossils were related – as Lamarck had suggested – to living animals; whether there was a sequence of development from one to another; and whether particular fossils were contemporaneous or not.

In September 1832, at Punta Alta on the coast of Argentina, Darwin found remains of a huge *Megatherium* 'great animal'. *Megatherium* had been known since 1789 and had been beautifully described by Cuvier as a member of the sloth family, big as a rhinoceros. It was clear evidence of an animal that 'revolutions of the globe seem to have destroyed'. In 1833, Darwin found more fossils, bits of an animal Richard Owen named *Glyptodon* 'curved tooth'. Not only were its teeth extraordinary but it also had an amazing spiked club at the end of its tail. But its scaly armour and general structure reminded Darwin of modern armadillos. If there were a relationship, it was necessary to establish the time factor.

Darwin had been speculating on contemporaneity in 1832. He had asked whether the bones of his monster fossils were coexistent with present-day shell species or whether they antedated them. Complicating the solution to this problem was whether the fossils as he found them were in their 'proper' place or whether they had been washed out of some other stratum more ancient or more modern. He asked himself this in his notebook and promised himself he would examine the structure of the rocks more closely. All this was as exciting to Darwin as shells found three miles up a mountain. It turned out that *Megatherium* and *Glyptodon* – and Darwin's new discovery of the giant *Toxodon* 'bow tooth' – had co-existed with recent fossils of still-surviving shell species. 'Great animal', 'curved tooth' and 'bow tooth' were not that old but they had become extinct. More exciting was a horse tooth, recognizably horse but subtly different from modern horse.

Lyell – Darwin's textbook – did not, of course, interpret fossils as evidence of succession and transmutation. Lyell believed that all basic types of animals had been present since the original creation but species and varieties had appeared and disappeared from time to time as the environment changed. The only reason that mammals and birds had not been found in the earliest rocks was, according to Lyell, because they were not as tough as shells and, consequently, had not survived the fossilization process.

Darwin was finding it difficult to follow Lyell. The monster fossils might be extinct and unrepresentative of anything alive today but remains of armadillos in the caves of Brazil – and the horse tooth – were surely evidence of direct relationship, even ancestry.

These thoughts continued without any immediate solution. Even after the outflow of geological articles and books on his return to England he was not ready to solve the problem of fossils. So, in the 1840s, Darwin turned to a study of barnacles which – like all Darwin's little studies – grew into a major undertaking. Barnacles occupied him for seven years: *A Monograph of the Fossil Lepadidae; or Pedunculated Cirripedes of*

Great Britain appeared in 1851. Fossil barnacles could be traced through the rock strata and gradual changes could be seen in them. They were splendid illustrations of progressive evolution. But Darwin – although by then convinced of evolution and his own explanation of it – was not yet ready to reveal his secret. The barnacles were tantalizing evidence. There was abundant evidence that the sessile barnacles – like the common acorn barnacle of British coasts – had existed in large numbers through many rock formations during the Tertiary or Cenozoic era (the last 65 million years). It was strange, therefore, to find no remains in rocks of the Secondary or Mesozoic era – from 65 to 245 million years ago – or earlier. They might have appeared suddenly. They did not conform to Lyell's theory that everything had always been in existence nor did they conform to Darwin's increasing commitment to gradualism and transmutation. The most obvious interpretation was creation. The fossil barnacles seemed to refute the evolutionary ideas that he dared not print. But his patience was rewarded. He was sent a drawing one day of a barnacle fossil from an old rock stratum that provided an ancestor for his more recent ones. Barnacles, after all, would provide an example of succession in the geological record for his great work on evolution – *Natural Selection*.

Chapter 9 of the *Origin* – 'On the Imperfection of the Geological Record' – was a formidable array of geological facts that Darwin called the 'evidence for evolution'. He described how the earth had been formed by processes of uplift and subsidence, by water erosion and by volcanoes. He referred to his map of coral reefs as evidence for subsidence in modern oceans. He gave the Weald as an example of denudation by water. He explained sedimentation. He pointed out that the forces that formed the earth varied from place to place and from time to time: some sediments were thick, some were thin; some land had been elevated, some tilted; some parts subsided relative to other parts and sank into formations like the Craven fault in

Shropshire. Everything Darwin observed conformed to Lyell's interpretation of a gradually evolving earth.

Fossils should provide equivalent evidence of evolving animals but, unfortunately, the fossil record had gaps. Strata might not become exposed and organisms might not become fossilized. Along the west coast of America, Darwin noticed hardly any Tertiary formations so that 'no record of several successive and peculiar marine faunas will probably be preserved.' The ancestral barnacle that suddenly turned up and filled a gap indicated that other 'missing links' might turn up. Such chance events – and whether excavations were in the right place – could account for the 'abrupt manner in which whole groups of species suddenly appear in certain formations'.

The chapter ended with the conclusion that fossils formed a sequence of evolutionary change but that the record was imperfect and always would be. But it was evidence of evolution and not, he thought, evidence of creation or catastrophe. He admitted it was rash to differ from such 'great authorities' and 'eminent palaeontologists' as Cuvier, Murchison, Agassiz and Sedgwick. Sedgwick still believed in creation. Lyell, too, was against organic transmutation. But Darwin's opposition to Lyell was formulated in Lyellian terms and explicitly followed 'Lyell's metaphor' in describing the natural geological record – and its fossils – as a 'history of the world imperfectly kept'. The idea had been in his head since the first fossil finds in South America.

Chapter 10 of the *Origin* – 'On the Geological Succession of Organic Beings' – provided sophisticated interpretations of fossil relationships – like *Megatherium* and modern sloths – and of the causes of extinction. Extinctions, he argued, were not evidence of global catastrophes but local events caused by many different factors. The fossil horse tooth he had found was evidence of gradual extinction caused by changing climate and vegetation. Other animals might have been rare – and rarity frequently led to extinction – but Darwin gave no example. Competition could lead to extinction. Competition between fish could have been the cause of many groups disappearing from the sea. Sudden extinctions might be explained by the sudden immigration of new species which competed successfully with the old. 'Thus, as it seems to me,' he concluded, 'the manner in which single and whole groups of species become extinct, accords well with the theory of natural selection.' Continuity and relationship were more likely than catastrophic extinction and creation.

Fossils and their living relatives raised another problem: was climate or relationship the cause of similarity?

Throughout Patagonia, the flora and fauna were striking in the uniform adaptation to arid conditions: the dwarf plants, the insects, the birds, the huge herds of guanaco, the rodents – existing without water – and the puma. A footnote in the second edition of the *Journal*, in 1845, compared Patagonia with the Syrian desert. In Syria, uniform dwarf bushes and small rodents: but instead of guanacos, gazelles; and instead of agoutis, hares. Why, he asked, should desert inhabitants differ if they had been created for the same conditions? And why was the fauna of South America more like that of North America in the past – the comparatively recent past – than today?

Those *Megatherium* ground sloths and the related *Megalonyx* 'big claw' and *Mylodon* 'grinding tooth' from Punta Alta had also been found in rocks of North America. And North America had remains of elephants, mastodons and horses. 'The more I reflect on this case, the more interesting it appears,' he admitted to his *Journal*. If North America and South America had had such similarity in the past, why had they become different? At first, it seemed just good evidence for Lyellian geology. The Mexican platform could have been elevated recently to form a barrier or the West Indies might have subsided. North America, anyway, was probably not the original home of elephants or mastodons for there are elephants in the Old World tropics today. Perhaps they came to the New World from the Old World across ancient land bridges which had become submerged in the Bering Straits. He was beginning to see an answer to Buffon's puzzle: the differences between Africa and South America, in spite of climatic similarities. Change, migration and replacement might be the answer when linked to a changing earth of barriers and bridges. Even the Andes in Chile might be important barriers for plants, he confided to a notebook in 1836.

Yet this was not the whole story. Many of the animals and plants of South America were unique. The guinea pigs and the tinamus and the heliconiid butterflies did not seem to be immigrants from North America. Why had they been created for South America and for nowhere else? And even more puzzling were the flora and fauna of the South American islands. By 1859, two chapters on 'Geographical Distribution' were serving as further evidence for evolution. Inevitably, he wrote, we are brought to the question of 'whether species have been created at one or more points of the earth's surface'. Had the rhea of La Plata been specially created for La Plata? Why not an ostrich as in Africa or an emu as in Australia? Why had the agoutis and vizcachas been preferred to the hares and rabbits of the north? The simplicity of a creationist view, he admitted, 'captivated the mind'. But, he continued, it seemed to him that species had been formed from pre-existing species, had evolved and migrated, mixed and replaced each other and finally arrived at their present shape and place. Differences in climate and physical barriers would modify the details but, on the whole, neighbouring land masses would be more similar to each other than widely separated land masses: the deserts of North and South America more alike, than either to the Syrian desert.

But how did animals get from one place to another? They could move slowly across land: taking advantage of land connections, stopping where barriers were insurmountable. But, Darwin thought, a lot of migration must have taken place across seemingly inhospitable barriers. How else to account for island faunas and floras? Seeds might float in the sea without losing their capacity to germinate, might stick to floating timber, or become entangled in a bird's feathers or stuck in the mud on a bird's foot. A snail's eggs might stick to floating seaweed. He had seen stranded logs on island beaches and on the coasts of New Holland. By the time dispersal came to be incorporated in the *Origin* Darwin had experimented with asparagus seeds and hazel nuts and found they would germinate after months of floating in water. Two papers on the results of his experiments had been published in 1855 and 1856. Freeze the seeds and they could still survive. Icebergs and glaciers, therefore, were another possible means of transport.

Dispersal by wind, dispersal by water, dispersal by ice and dispersal by other organisms distributed animals and plants to islands from continents and even from continent to continent. There was a pattern: a pattern that argued for natural causes, even in this apparently accidental process. The direction of the winds, the direction of the ocean currents, the nearness of land determined which seeds, which eggs, would be carried to any particular island. Darwin visualized mountain tops as islands – in an expanse of lowland – with seeds and insects blowing from mountain top to mountain top, crossing the inhospitable spaces in between. In this, Darwin differed from Wallace. Wallace preferred to think of mountain species as isolated remnants of a former wide and continuous distribution, a distribution broken up by earth movements or climatic changes. Hooker – on whom Darwin relied for many plant examples – was also in favour of widespread distribution and subsequent fragmentation but he went further than Wallace and advocated former land bridges to account for discontinuities. He did not believe the dispersal of plants across great wastes of ocean was a useful explanation for the strange distribution of plants on the southern continents. It was particularly difficult to see how it could explain the similarities of the floras of south-west Australia and the Cape of Good Hope. And, with that, Darwin had to agree. But Darwin did not accept Hooker's antarctic bridge hypothesis for such a distribution. He left the question open.

Mountains might be a problem but islands in the sea did not

cause any disagreement between Darwin and Wallace: there were islands of volcanic origin, oceanic islands; and there were islands that had become separated from a land mass by subsidence or rise in sea level, continental islands. There was no doubt in Darwin's mind that the oceanic Galapagos Islands had been colonized from South America by transoceanic and aerial transport. There was no doubt in Wallace's mind that the fauna from St Helena had come mainly on the north-westerly ocean currents from the southern coast of Africa. Whatever the source, island faunas were evidence of speciation. Island faunas – the tortoises and finches of the Galapagos and the parrots and swallowtail butterflies of Celebes – had not been specially created. Island faunas were astonishing. Small differences in shape and colour of finch or butterfly on neighbouring islands made no sense in terms of creation. They made sense only if the islands were colonized from nearby land, the colonists isolated and trimmed for the new surroundings by natural selection.

When Darwin reached the Galapagos Islands, in September 1835, he was already a seasoned naturalist but not even Darwin could have expected the effect that visit would have on his thoughts. He had been looking forward to the Galapagos if only because – as he wrote to his sister – the islands were on the *Beagle*'s way home. The South American coast and its waters had been carefully charted: there was nothing more to do except sail home across the Pacific and Indian Oceans.

Unfortunately, Darwin's letters from the Galapagos Islands to Caroline have not survived and, referring to the islands in a later letter, he describes them merely as 'a land of craters'. An entry in one of the ornithological notebooks for 7 September 1835 reported a collection of birds from the islands of the archipelago and commented that the Spaniards had known which island a tortoise came from by the shape, size and pattern of its carapace: 'If there is the slightest foundation for these remarks,' he concluded, 'the Zoology of the Archipelagoes will be well worth examining; for such facts would undermine the stability of species.' Such a heterodox interpretation of island faunas did not appear again until the *Origin* when he argued that speciation on a group of islands – where each species was more closely related to its nearest neighbours than to any other species in any other part of the world – was just what would be expected on a theory of speciation by natural selection and not at all what would be expected from a belief in creation.

There were damp woods on the Galapagos but there were neither frogs nor toads. Surprising, Darwin thought, until he remembered that Jean Baptiste Bory St Vincent had noticed that volcanic islands far out in the ocean never had amphibia and he himself had seen none on the Cape Verde Islands. The explanation could only be that the unprotected eggs would be unlikely to make a sea crossing. How could creation explain the omission?

In the journal of the *Beagle*, Darwin described the geology and biology of the Galapagos Islands. He described their volcanic origin. He marvelled at the prickly-pear trees, huge tortoises, iguanas and the incredible and unique marine iguanas feeding on seaweed. Nowhere else had an iguana been discovered swimming in the sea. It was unique but, at the same time, it was clearly related to the terrestrial iguanas and to iguanas far away in America. The *Journal* was packed with descriptions built up from the almost indiscriminate collections and observations of the young naturalist. Everything interested him. To add to the island speciation of giant tortoises was 'a most singular group of finches'. Islands had their own species of finch, differing slightly in colour but more dramatically in the size and shape of beak. There were finches with long beaks, finches with short beaks, finches with nutcracker beaks and finches in between. Darwin's finch collection amounted to thirteen species when it was described by Gould. Galapagos finches seemed to be adapted to different ways of feeding, according to the circumstances in which they found themselves: the availability of certain foods; the lack of certain competitors and predators. In the *Journal*,

Darwin risked a mild version of the entry he had made in his ornithological notebook. 'One might really fancy', he wrote, 'that from an original paucity of birds in this archipelago, one species had been taken and modified for different ends.' This was softened further a few pages later: 'There must be an astonishing amount of creative force if such an expression may be used.' He was certainly not yet prepared to share his secret thoughts with the public. But, in hindsight, the *Beagle* journal is sprinkled with suggestive comments about the continental affinities of the Galapagos fauna and its adaptive modification to different circumstances. At the time, no one seemed to notice the hints except perhaps Wallace who had read and enjoyed the *Journal* long before setting out for South America 'with a view to study the origin of species'.

3. A Natural System

'Naturalists try to arrange the species, genera, and families in each class, on what is called the Natural System. But what is meant by this system?' Darwin 1859.

Darwin had been taken on board the *Beagle* as a naturalist. He was recommended as 'amply qualified for collecting, observing and noting anything worthy to be noted in Natural History'; or, as Darwin described himself, 'some scientific person'. Geology made its impression on him early in the voyage, coming immediately as it did after his initiation with Sedgwick in North Wales and his reading of the first volume of Lyell's *Principles*. The conflicting opinions of the two famous geologists stimulated the young naturalist as he sailed from one new geological phenomenon to another, from volcanic island to rising coastline, from breccia to clay, from *Megatherium* to mastodon. Who was right? Cuvier and Sedgwick? Or Lyell? If, as seemed likely, it was Lyell, then he must convince himself by observation. The questioning and the corroboration occupied him throughout the voyage.

Not that Darwin neglected his duties as a collector of living specimens. He was out with his net sweeping the shores and the plains at every opportunity, bringing in groups of insects from unlikely places: thirteen species of insect from an island off the Chile coast. His beloved beetles abounded: sixty-eight species from Rio de Janeiro from one day's collecting in June 1832; and – to show that he was not merely indulging his own interests – thirty-seven species of arachnid.

Masses of zoological and botanical specimens came on board the *Beagle* to be added, eventually, to the nation's store in the British Museum. He had to keep control over all those specimens. Put a number on every specimen – he later advised the aspiring naturalist – and catalogue it immediately. Never trust anything to memory: thus, the collector would avoid the 'otherwise inevitable future anxiety of uncertainty'. He dried, he pressed, he skinned, he bottled and he noted what he saw. There were new species of cactus from scorching plains, strange orchids growing parasitically on decaying tree trunks, beautiful butterflies, brilliant parrots, big vizcacha rodents and a burrowing barnacle.

Darwin described few of his own specimens. An early paper on the South American rhea was an exception. 'Ostrich' hunting on the Argentinian plains appealed to his sporting habits and he had become familiar with the flocks of *Rhea americana*. But when a small dark bird was shot near the Straits of Magellan he was only just quick enough to salvage – for the Zoological Society in London – the bits and pieces from the pot. It was a new species – *Rhea darwinii* – which he described in 1837.

Darwin's magpie's collection of scattered finds provided an overview of each area he visited rather than an in-depth contribution to any particular group of plants or animals. Everything turned up, sooner or later. Much of it was new to science: from the huge thigh bones of *Mylodon darwinii* to Darwin's 'American partridge', the tinamu *Nothura darwinii*; and from the Galapagos rice rat *Oryzomys darwinii* – and the Chilean leaf-eared mouse *Phyllotis darwinii* – to the Patagonian iguana *Diplolaenus darwinii*, running across the hot stones of the inhospitable Patagonian plains. New species of plants, too, came on board to be stored in the *Beagle*'s hold: from the dry shingle wastes, *Opuntia darwinii*, Darwin's prickly pear; from the forests of Tierra del Fuego, the edible honey fungus *Cyttaria darwinii*.

Relationships – similarities – were emerging from the collections: the relationship of the giant armadillo fossil with the modern armadillo, trotting over the sand dunes of Bahia Blanca, looking for beetles 'so quiet' that it seemed 'almost a pity to kill such nice little animals'; and the relationship of the 'nice little animals' with sloths; relationships between marine iguanas and terrestrial iguanas; relationships between Galapagos animals and American animals. Darwin incorporated such observations as he hammered away at the evidence for evolution. Chapter 13 of the *Origin* was on 'Mutual Affinities of Organic Beings: Morphology: Embryology: Rudimentary Organs'.

Classification was about relationships. It arranged living organisms in an hierarchical system. And classification was about differences as well as similarities.

Darwin had tried his hand at classification during the years between his geological works and the *Origin*. He had described and named barnacles according to 'the rules', which he found 'very useful'. He told Hugh Strickland, zoologist and expert on nomenclature, on 29 January 1849: 'It is quite a comfort to have something to rest on in the turbulent ocean of nomenclature . . . though I find it very difficult to obey always.'

The rules of nomenclature were laid down by Carl Linnaeus in the tenth edition of *Systema Naturae* (1758). Naturalists had always classified: in order to talk about organisms, in order to identify finds. Some had looked beyond the utilitarianism of the system, searching to discover a pattern in nature, the Divine Plan. Thus, Aristotle's pattern was a ladder, the *scala naturae*. It was based on differences between animals: animals with red blood and animals without red blood; animals with eight legs, six legs, four legs, two legs and no legs; or different types of reproduction. It put whales in a special group near fish, sea urchins with snails. There had been little advance on Aristotle's classification. But the need for improvement became obvious when botanists like John Ray tried to establish a dichotomous key: to identify the mass of new material pouring into Europe as more and more travellers reached the 'ends of the world' and sent back specimens. The keys became chaotic: order was called for. The order was provided by Linnaeus who – while advocating a natural system of classification which would reveal relationships – decided on an artificial one because too little was known of the

natural one. Convenience should override all other consider-
ations. Linnaeus decided to group organisms according to
constant characters and chose the reproductive organs as the
most important since that was how species were perpetuated. He
invented a new vocabulary to describe categories of classification.
Thus, species came to have two names: the generic name and the
specific name.

No one attempted to change the Linnean nomenclature – in
spite of the artificiality of the system – but there were many
attempts in the nineteenth century to find the natural
classification that Linnaeus had advocated but not found.
Lamarck expressed the opinion that the Aristotelian emphasis
on differences was the wrong approach. Lamarck saw living
organisms as a series with no rigidly defined boundaries between
groups. Interesting, theoretically, but not a useful concept for
the museum taxonomist. Lamarck divided animals into invertebrates and vertebrates: getting away, for the first time, from
the basic Aristotelian criterion of blood. Lamarck arranged the
animal kingdom in sixteen classes of ascending complexity but –
in spite of his opinion about emphasizing similarities rather than
dissimilarities – used many negative characters in his classification, in the Aristotle–Linnaeus tradition: thus, worms had no
legs; molluscs, no spinal cord. And he more or less accepted –
regardless of his commitment to evolution – Cuvier's system of
classification. For Cuvier, a natural system must reveal essences.
Find the constant characters of a group – like the nervous system
– and find the essence of that group. Characters of the individual
animal – like organs – maintained the needs – and, thus, the
essence – of the animal. The beaks of birds were modified to eat a
special type of food in order to maintain the special essence of
bird. The form of one organ was correlated with the form of
another and when everything was ordered to show those
correlations it would be possible to predict the essence of an
animal from parts of its anatomy. Prediction from essences and
correlation of parts was a useful system for a palaeontologist like

Cuvier trying to identify a fossil from a few bits and pieces. The groupings he obtained from applying his system led him to formulate *embranchements* as the basic arrangement of creation. Animals could be put into one of four *embranchements*, similar to today's phyla. The *embranchements* were separate acts of creation. Within them, smaller groups had been created. Individuals within groups might vary but it was limited and did not lead to change. Such variation upset the co-ordinated whole and would be eliminated. Any 'selection' there might be would inevitably lead to stability. It was the differences – the uncrossable gaps – that were emphasized.

The Cuvierian system of classification, with the Linnean nomenclature, was an acceptable system for a nineteenth-century biologist. It was more or less the system according to which Darwin's specimens were classified at the British Museum.

When Darwin began work on classification he insisted that he had 'originally intended to have described only a single abnormal Cirripede [barnacle] from the shores of South America' but – once he got going – 'I was led, for the sake of comparison, to examine the internal parts of as many genera as I could procure.' He examined his own collection of barnacles and had access to the British Museum collections. He borrowed private collections; and biologists, like Agassiz and Milne-Edwards, sent him the odd fresh specimen from time to time. He inspected each barnacle with care and no detail of ornamentation on the shells eluded him. He dissected each organ system and was allowed to dissect unique specimens from other collections. He found chaos in the systematics of the group. Almost every species had to be redescribed, regrouped and even renamed. It was a major task. He asked friends to invent names for new species he described but refused to put his own name after a description – in the conventional way – 'as if some merit was due to a man for merely naming and describing a species'.

Darwin wanted to give an idea of the 'history' of the group by his reclassification. Disdain for mere description neither dulled his perception nor sapped his perseverance. He bought a new microscope to look at the tiny 'parasites' that clung inside the shells and found they looked like barnacles. Surely, he reasoned, a parasitic barnacle would not be tolerated fitting snugly inside another barnacle. As far as he could see, the 'parasites' had small shells, prehensile antennae and male reproductive organs typical of barnacles. They seemed to have no mouth or gut and, however hard he looked, he could find no female reproductive organs. He called the 'parasites' complemental males.

To find a minute male in a big female barnacle was not that surprising, in fact: such things were known in the wheel animalcules, the rotifers. But why were there tiny males in species of hermaphrodite barnacle? That was a discovery but also a puzzle he could not solve. But the discovery might fit neatly into the facts he was assembling for his argument about the origin of species. One way of interpreting the peculiar sexual arrangements of barnacles was to think in terms of *progression* of species: from hermaphrodites to hermaphrodites with complemental males, then to separately sexed barnacles. There must be some reason why some genera had those sexual arrangements but, for the moment, the most he would say in print was: 'I infer there must be some profounder and more mysterious final cause.' He explained it – to Hooker – in a different way: 'you will perhaps wish my barnacles and species theory at Diavolo together' (1848).

The identification and classification of the barnacles – leading to the discovery of the complemental males – was an example of the way in which Darwin worked. Nothing was too trivial, nothing was too time-consuming. If there were anomalies, then more specimens had to be investigated until the norm was discovered. Variations in barnacles were as much the raw material of selection as variation in pigeons.

With the barnacle monograph, Darwin considered he had advanced. He was now a professional zoologist as well as a professional geologist. Authority would be important when he revealed his inner thoughts.

For the moment, he was content to follow 'the rules': 'on true Baconian principles, and without any theory [I] collected facts on a wholesale scale.' He collected facts on a wholesale scale but it would be naïve to believe he worked without a theory. All his geological studies tested the truth of Lyell's principles against Cuvier's catastrophes. His natural history was selected to show adaptation, variation, dispersal and isolation. Barnacles had fitted into a theory of descent with modification. Barnacles had turned out to be descendant crustaceans: even though 'the illustrious Cuvier did not perceive that a barnacle was, as it certainly is, a Crustacean'; and even though Richard Owen would not accept such a relationship. Barnacles were modified crustaceans: the crustacean's limbs modified into food-gathering cirri, the crustacean ovarian tube modified into an adhesive organ.

The barnacle study provided Darwin with material for a section in the *Origin*. New rules for classification were laid down in the *Origin* as well as classification itself being used as evidence for evolution. The barnacle study showed the necessity of classifying on groups of characters: 'the value indeed of an aggregate of characters is very evident in natural history.' But he would follow Cuvier in 'weighting' characters differently. Whatever character of a plant or animal was most constant – and, therefore, the less concerned with special habits – was the most important for classification. But did not weighting and the realization that there were some constant and some variable characters argue in favour of common ancestry? Or was it variation round an essence or an archetype? Darwin was against the archetype theory because he had found that an organ might be serving one function in one group of animals but be modified to serve another function in another group. Moreover, characters and their modifications often revealed a chain of affinities. There were crustaceans, he argued, at opposite ends of a chain that had almost no characters in common yet there were other species – in between – which provided a link. What pattern, then, did careful classification reveal? Did it reveal a plan of creation? It revealed a tree irregularly branched – 'the coral of life' – as Darwin illustrated, in his 1837 species notebook. A new natural classification was emerging.

The construction of natural chains – trees or corals – was based on an assessment of homologies: of similarities rather than differences; positive features rather than negative. Homology had been used by the exponents of archetype classification to find the essence of a group. Homology had even become a curious anatomical game in which parts of an animal were homologized with other parts of the same animal, the most famous example of which was serial homology of the vertebral column. Each vertebra was homologous with each other vertebra and, finally, with the skull: *'Der Mensch ist ein Wirbel'* – 'man is a vertebra' – Goethe proclaimed as he held aloft a skull picked up casually in a graveyard. For Darwin, serial homology said little: it could not apply to molluscs which were not segmented; it was not, therefore, a universal phenomenon. For Darwin, the search for homologies was a search for relationships: for the community of descent which 'is the hidden bond which naturalists have been unconsciously seeking' and which would make sense of classification. Darwin thought descent from a remote ancestor with unspecialized swimming appendages was a better explanation of the specialized mouthparts of a crab than metaphysical essences and serial homology.

Descent with modification could also make sense of the widespread existence of rudimentary organs. There were beetles with rudimentary wings – everyone agreed the rudiments represented wings – and there were rudimentary pistils in the male florets of daisies. The horse and the ox had rudimentary toes, like Buffon's pig. The kiwi had rudimentary wings. The ovigerous frena (sticky anchors) of some barnacles were rudimentary: no longer used for attaching ova. Apparently useless, the frena were still there and – even more extraordinary – available for natural selection to turn them into gills in other species. The only possible explanation was evolution which avoids 'the strange difficulty' they would present 'on the ordinary doctrine of creation'.

But beware of analogies as distinct from homologies, Darwin warned. Had not Lamarck already identified the problem of distinguishing between organs looking alike because they performed similar functions and looking alike because they had the same ancestry? (This was the only mention of Lamarck in the *Origin*.) Was it not this confusion that had classified whales near fish, the South American vizcachas with Australian marsupials?

One way of sorting out the problem – like whether a barnacle was a mollusc or a crustacean – was to look at the embryology of the animals because the embryos often bore a greater resemblance to each other than the adults. Vaughan Thompson first suggested the crustacean affinities of barnacles because of the similarity of their larvae. Von Baer's extensive studies of vertebrate development showed that similarities between embryos gradually became less as the embryos developed into the adult form: into fish, reptile or bird. Von Baer's observations were well known in England, having been used by Owen to show the hierarchical structure of the animal kingdom culminating in man. Several palaeontologists, including Hugh Miller and Agassiz, linked the fossil sequence with embryonic development. The author of the *Vestiges* had claimed that the insect larva represented its worm-like past, the intermaxillary bone of man his ape ancestry.

Miller and Agassiz were no evolutionists: in spite of embryological analogies with the fossil record, each group had its special creation. For the author of the *Vestiges*, the similarities provided evidence of evolution by recapitulation, a theory which was to triumph in the hands of Ernst Haeckel: that an amphibian embryo went through all the stages of becoming an adult fish before becoming an adult amphibian. Von Baer did not believe that fish were ancestral to amphibia – he was no evolutionist – and merely stated that vertebrate embryos look more like each other than do the adults.

With those facts to draw on, Darwin set to work on the larval forms and metamorphosis of barnacles, work which provided a considerable part of his argument for evolution in Chapter 13. He studied all the barnacle larvae he could get and he confirmed that the larvae were indeed like crustacean larvae: 'I feel much confidence, that the homologies here given are correct.' They had just been overlooked. At metamorphosis, the three pairs of legs of the typical crustacean larva were converted into prehensile cirri, extending into the water to fish for food. The parasitic *Proteolepas* was a case of arrested development. It never arrived at the stage when a shell would be formed. Who would recognize it for a barnacle unless they had studied its larva? What if other organisms provided equally good evidence?

Darwin looked at newly hatched pigeons. He measured the proportions of beak, mouth, legs and feet and found that all were similar whatever the breed. The earlier the stage of development, the more the chicks resembled each other, just as von Baer had shown. Darwin had read von Baer's essays in 1850 but he did not refer to them in the *Origin* and, contrary to von Baer, Darwin concluded that 'community of embryonic structures reveals community of descent'. One more point was made.

Through his own observations, Darwin brought the evidence of morphology, rudimentary organs, homology and embryology to bear on the question of evolution. Thus, he argued not only that the facts supported a theory of common descent but also that they provided a basis for 'a natural system of classification'.

Darwin's natural system of classification differed from those of his predecessors in several ways. His system was not strictly hierarchical in the Linnean sense because his system branched. Tips of branches could be equivalent to one another. In the Linnean system, organisms were either above or below one another. In principle, Darwin's system rejected dissimilarities or negative characters as criteria for classification: 'no legs' was not a useful discriminatory characteristic. (Today, classification still uses 'invertebrates'.) Grouping by positive similarities would be the basis of a natural system that would provide evidence that a group of species 'had descended from one ancient but unseen parent, and consequently, have inherited something in common'. Darwin did not get rid of negative criteria, in practice: he resorted to it in the barnacle classification. But he was out to show that his thesis of branching evolution was confirmed by organisms classified according to similarities. He was not about to reclassify the animal kingdom.

The barnacle work had occupied a lot of time between 1846 and 1854 and delayed the development of the 1844 essay into the *Origin*. But it provided an excuse for not rushing into print on a subject Darwin knew to be dynamite – and it provided time to think over the evolution problem – and it 'got out of the way' the South American burrowing barnacle. In September 1854 – once the barnacle work was out of the way – Darwin sent 10,000 barnacles back to the owners. Nothing was ever heard of the 'beloved barnacles' again: except for a brief appearance in the *Origin*; and in a one-page paper on the so-called auditory sac of barnacles, in 1863.

The circumstantial evidence for evolution – geological record, distribution of living organisms, mutual affinities – occupied the closing chapters of the *Origin*. He had drawn on his own experience, his own experiments and his own anatomical research and he had added an immense amount of factual material drawn from his voracious reading and his extensive correspondence. Nothing further of any consequence was published on those subjects. They had served their purpose as supporting evidence and further development was left to others. He put all those 'innumerable well-observed facts stored in the minds of naturalists' into their 'proper places'.

Earlier chapters of the *Origin* still held intriguing questions.

4. Variation and Inheritance

'But I am strongly inclined to suspect that the most frequent cause of variability may be attributed to the male and female reproductive elements having been affected prior to the act of conception,' Darwin 1859.

The first pages of the *Origin* were on the causes of variability without which natural selection could not effect changes. The rest of the chapter provided evidence of variability and the effective changes brought about by human selection in domestic animals. The second chapter took up variability in natural populations.

First Darwin had to sort out the difference between a species and a variety. Varieties occurred within a species but, in the nineteenth century, the two terms were often interchangeable. Look, he said, at the dozen or so varieties of oak tree: all of them had been called species in their time; and yet not more than one or two of them could be called a species in its own right – the rest were local varieties, the material for selection. In the second chapter, he tried to define a species but was forced to the conclusion that the only way to decide whether something was a species or a variety was to ask 'the opinion of naturalists having sound judgement and wide experience'. But the very existence of the problem provided evidence that there was variation in wild populations. And it was all round him in the fields of Kent – exactly as it had been in the Galapagos Archipelago.

Varieties within a species were the main evidence for variation, though he did not ignore individual differences between members of a population or family. He quoted reports on individual variation in insect musculature and the existence in human populations of albino and hairy individuals in otherwise normal families. He observed the variation due to polymorphism: the existence of two or more distinct forms without any intermediates in the same population; but polymorphism puzzled him. He suspected the forms of being neither advantageous nor disadvantageous for selection but neutral. He shelved the problem. But it was all good evidence for variation. Nevertheless, he settled on variation in domestic animals for his evidence.

Everyone could appreciate it in pigeons: the long tails, the short tails, the fan tails and so on; in sheep with long fleeces and sheep with short; and the King Charles spaniel and the pointer. Working on chance appearance of desirable variations, men had selectively bred for animals with those characters. It could be imagined that this was how selection worked in nature.

Variation abounded but what was the cause? He had gathered a considerable amount of material on variation – and the possible causes of variation – for the unpublished volumes of *Natural Selection* but he reduced it all to three chapters in the *Origin*; and he had not found a cause. On 7 January 1860 – two days after the publication of the second edition of the *Origin* – Darwin started to go over his notes on variation and worked steadily until May. He considered all the possible causes of variation. One clue, he believed, lay in sexual reproduction. When primroses and cowslips bloomed at Down he examined them carefully and found that some had flowers with long stamens and short pistils, others flowers with short stamens and long pistils. He decided to call the first, male plants – because he thought long stamens would produce a lot of pollen – while the others with the long pistils (and a rough stigma) would be the better seed producers and he called them female plants. He seemed to have found a parallel to the barnacles: a transition from one type of sexual arrangement to another, from hermaphrodite plants to plants with differentiated male and female plants. He began experiments and found, almost at once, that he was wrong. The two forms of *Primula* were stable forms, not forms in transition – in process of evolving. The existence of two forms ensured cross-fertilization and cross-fertilization was brought about by insects.

Polymorphism ensured cross-fertilization. He reported his findings in 1862. Careful observation had once more led to a discovery.

Meanwhile the projected *The Variation of Animals and Plants under Domestication* (1868) was not making much progress: only three chapters written by the time Darwin went on holiday to Torquay in the summer of 1861.

In Torquay, he became fascinated by orchids and, for the rest of the year, the fertilization of orchids was his obsession. He sought to understand the meaning of the shapes of the flowers and, by meticulous observation, discovered that, like *Primula*, they were 'co-adapted for fertilization by insects and, therefore, the results of natural selection'. The work grew into a book, *The Various Contrivances by which Orchids are Fertilised by Insects*, published in 1862. It was to complement the *Origin*: a new example of natural selection at work; and it was particularly important because it demonstrated the interactions between quite different organisms.

Orchids was also important for Darwin's self-esteem. It proved, he hoped, that he was now a professional botanist because, as he told his publisher, it showed he had 'worked hard at details'. The fossils and geology of South American islands had established his reputation as a geologist, barnacles had established his zoological competence and *Orchids* – though three years after the publication of the *Origin* – seemed to him necessary to establish his botanical competence. *Orchids* was only the first of many botanical publications.

He delighted in seeing all round him the variation in form of the products of natural selection. His theory was proving a stimulus to further work and further work was confirming his theory.

The pyramidal orchid *Orchis pyramidalis* grew abundantly at Down and was one of his favourite flowers, astonishing in the complexity of its adaptations for cross-fertilization by Lepidoptera, both by day and by night. The bright purple colour attracted day-flying moths, the strong foxy odour attracted night-fliers. On arrival they were accurately guided to the long nectary by sloping ridges on the lip of the corolla. Anyone could test this, he wrote, by inserting a bristle – representing the proboscis of the moth – into the nectary. But the mouth of the nectary was overhung by a rostellum, forming a trap-door. On either side was a stigma and, above, there were two anther bags of pollen with sticky discs. The moth withdrew its tongue and the discs stuck to the moth, contracting when they reached the air, so that the bags curled round the proboscis. Darwin timed it – thirty seconds – and during those seconds the moth was well on its way to the next flower to complete the cross-fertilization. To prove the point, Darwin inspected the proboscises of several species of moth and butterfly and found pollen bags stuck to them; and he covered flowers to prevent access by insects and the flowers set no seeds. But what was most surprising was that the bee orchid *Ophrys apifera* was self-fertilized – as Darwin again proved by experiment – and yet it still had the same complicated flower of other British *Ophrys* which were cross-fertilized by insects. Close examination, however, revealed that, through slight modifications of shape and size, the parts were perfectly adapted to self-fertilization by the wind. Wind blowing on the delicate elastic supports of the pollen bags brought them into contact with the stigma. Why, then, did the bee orchid look like a bee? Darwin decided that it did not and had only been given its name because of its fluffy lip and by analogy with the fly orchid which was, indeed, fertilized by flies and mimicked them.

Under the beech trees at Down grew the helleborine orchid *Cephalanthena* with yet another trick. Instead of nectar, coloured ridges attracted insects to chew them.

Having described the British orchids, Darwin went on to the exotics. He bought from dealers and he wrote to experts all over the world; and, like barnacles, orchids poured into Down. South American *Cattleyas* proved comparatively simple, shaped for a visiting bumble bee to take away pollen stuck to its back.

Angraecum had a long nectary so Darwin guessed, correctly, that it must be adapted for the elongated proboscis of a hawk moth in their native Madagascar. The orange-spotted *Catasetum* shot its pollen bags at insects standing on its lip – or in Darwin's face if he got in the way. But what pollinated *Cryptophenanthus* (*Mesdevallia*) with only its two tiny windows for access was not solved.

Catasetum had other claims to fame, apart from shooting pollen into Darwin's face. It seemed to be exclusively male. No anomaly like that could go unquestioned. Darwin inspected its nearest relatives and found that one was the female of the species, another an hermaphrodite; and the hermaphrodite was sterile. There, surely, was an orchid showing stages in the evolution of sex, from the hermaphrodite to the dioecious 'two houses' condition. Like barnacles, Darwin thought, the orchid's separate sexes were the evolutionary step from hermaphroditism.

Orchids were wonderfully graded in form, each form perfectly adapted to the conditions of existence: to attract a bee or a wasp and stick pollen on it; and receive pollen from another. And all parts of the flower were beautifully co-ordinated to effect pollination. Change the size and the shape changed, change the position of the pollen bags and the elasticity of the supports changed. Co-ordination of parts had echoes of Cuvier but, for Darwin, there could be no better demonstration of evolution: adaptation by natural selection, with modification of homologous parts for different functions. The subtle adaptations were more amazing than anything Darwin imagined possible. Those orchids that could not achieve cross-fertilization would disappear – would be selected out – and those that attracted a pollinator would survive.

The further conclusion must be that the fertilization mechanisms of orchids were a vivid demonstration of the importance of cross-fertilization. There must be, he argued, something injurious about self-fertilization and yet the bee orchid seemed to survive. Perhaps, he thought, it had once failed to be visited by its pollinator and, since any fertilization was better than none, had become adapted for self-fertilization. But could it resist the 'evil effects' of self-fertilization for ever? What were the relative merits of cross-fertilization and self-fertilization? Normally cross-fertilizing orchids made few seeds, normally self-fertilizing orchids a lot. Could it be that making pollen and seeds was so energy-consuming that the certainty of pollen delivery – however complex the adaptation – was an economy device?

Darwin had again delayed a great theoretical work for the sake of patient and detailed observation because – although he felt guilty about it – 'there is in me incomparably more interest in observing', he confessed to Asa Gray, 'than in writing' (July 1862).

Work was resumed on *Variation* and, by the end of 1866, it was nearly finished. But then another event occurred to distract Darwin. Gathering information for *Variation* and obsessed with finding a reason for cross-fertilization, he had sown, in his garden, two plots of toad flax *Linaria vulgaris*, one of which was cross-fertilized in the normal way, the other self-fertilized. To his astonishment – although both set seeds – the seedlings from the cross-fertilized plants grew more quickly and more vigorously than the seedlings from the self-fertilized plants. The same result was obtained with similar experiments on the clove pink *Dianthus caryophyllum*. Selection was again favouring plants adapted to cross-fertilization.

An account of the beneficial effects of cross-fertilization and the evident way in which cross-fertilization could be selected was incorporated into *Variation*. Hybrid plants were bigger and more vigorous than self-fertilized plants to which could be added examples from the animal world. Cross-breeding of sheep had been practised in England for years; and two varieties of pigeon could be crossed to produce a broader, tougher pigeon than either of its parents.

Three chapters of *Variation* discussed reproduction. Darwin was trying to unify the material: 'The existence of a great law of nature is, if not proved, at least rendered in the highest degree probable, namely that the crossing of animals and plants which are not closely related to each other is highly beneficial or even necessary and that inbreeding prolonged during many generations is highly injurious.'

The experiments still went on: the significance of cross-fertilization was still a puzzle. Years after the publication of *Variation*, Darwin was still searching for an explanation and for a good hypothesis to account for the origin of separate sexes. *The Effects of Cross and Self Fertilisation in the Vegetable Kingdom* was published in 1876. Orchids, toad flax, clove pinks and leguminous plants were brought to bear on the problem. Each holiday provided new data: there was wild thyme in Torquay, in 1861; foxgloves in Barmouth, in 1869. Assembled, the examples confirmed the vigour of cross-fertilized plants and gave him an idea on how to account for the evolution of separate sexes. Supposing, he argued, two plants of the same species, each adapted to slightly different conditions, came together on the same plot and cross-fertilization occurred. If the seedlings were especially vigorous, the arrangement would be favoured: being morphologically different, the two plants could become the male and female of the species, like those *Catasetum* orchids – where the male and female had been originally classified as separate genera.

It was not very satisfactory. More information was needed.

In *The Different Forms of Flowers on Plants of the Same Species* (1877) plants were grouped according to their adaptations for reproduction. There were heterostyled plants like the *Primula*, with alternative pin and thrum forms; and heterostyled plants with three forms, like loosestrife *Lythrum*. There were plants like lungwort *Pulmonaria* which had two sizes of pollen – Darwin measured it – but with seemingly no differentiation in the action; and there were plants like flax *Linum* which did not have size differentiated pollen – and yet the pollen was unable to make a pollen tube on its own stigma but made one readily on the stigma of another plant. There were plants that were dioecious, with separate and distinctive male and female flowers: either both on the same plant, like ash; or on separate plants, like holly. And there were plants that were either hermaphrodite or female, like thyme; and there were plants with two types of strikingly different flower, like *Viola* – one of which was cross-fertilized, the other self-fertilized.

There had to be an explanation of all that variety – of that polymorphism – which, since the *Origin*, had been 'very perplexing for they seem to show that this kind of variability is independent of the conditions of life'. Heterostyly and dioecy ensured cross-fertilization: cross-fertilization ensured vigorous seedlings and economized in pollen and ova. The self-fertilized flowers of *Viola*, tightly closed like buds, were adaptations to climate: the closed self-fertilizing flowers made more seed – like self-fertilizing orchids – than the cross-fertilized open flowers; and the seeds were produced only early in the season in some species, late in others; and, in others, only in some parts of the range. Thus, plants with the alternative of cross-fertilization and self-fertilization could occupy a wide range of environments. The reproductive arrangements were beautiful examples of adaptation for the conditions of existence. Polymorphism, he concluded with great satisfaction – at least in those examples – was an adaptation to different selective advantages in the environment.

Forms of Flowers gave Darwin more pleasure than any of his other books. He loved working on flowers and *Forms of Flowers* was full of practical advice to the horticulturalist. It was acclaimed for its guiding rules on plant breeding. The market gardener was instructed on how to ensure constancy of colour in the morning glory, petunia, carnation and monkey flower: by self-fertilization and careful control of the environment. Self-fertilization or inbreeding produced uniformity in the offspring – because inheritance had not been modified by cross-fertilization

– but only so long as the plants were cultivated in constant conditions.

Put plenty of pollen on the stigma when making the cross, Darwin advised: one pollen grain was not enough for fertilization. The literature had already, as he reported in Chapter 27 of *Variation*, provided that information. Had not Carl Gärtner found that more than forty pollen grains were needed to fertilize mallow *Malva*? Charles Naudin found that at least three pollen grains of the relatively huge pollen grains of 'marvel of Peru' *Mirabilis* were needed to produce an average number of seedlings. Darwin had tried himself, with several plants, but could not determine the exact amount needed.

Just as several pollen grains were required for plant fertilization so several spermatozoa were required for the fertilization of the egg of an animal. In *Variation*, Darwin reported the observations of Dr George Newport: that several spermatozoa were required to initiate the development of frogs' eggs; and J. L. A. de Quatrefages found a similar requirement in the shipworm *Teredo*. Thus, the actual amount of male contribution at fertilization was important: 'We must not overlook the effects of the unequal combination of the characters derived from both parents.' Large numbers of spermatozoa and pollen grains ensured vigorous embryos and seedlings.

But in 1830 Jean-Baptista Amici had watched down his microscope one pollen grain putting out a single pollen tube to grow down the style of an orchid and make contact with the egg cell. In 1856, the fusion of a single pollen nucleus with a single egg nucleus was observed and, in the same year, Nathaniel Pringsheim saw one spermatozoon enter the one egg cell of the freshwater alga *Odogonium*. So for all his voracious reading, for all Darwin's wide range of correspondents, he had not picked up those essential facts for interpreting inheritance.

Furthermore, Darwin believed in the age-old theory of blending.

At fertilization, juices mingled – or small particles mingled –

so that the offspring tended to be intermediate between the two parents. Both Joseph Kölreuter and Carl Gärtner had made hybrid plants – from tobacco to peas – that were intermediate between the parents, no matter which provided the pollen, which the ova. This was a major problem for Darwin. Inheritance had something to do with reproduction – he had established the importance of cross-fertilization – and yet because inherited factors fused, inheritance could only lead to uniformity. 'When individuals of the same variety, or even of a distinct variety, are allowed freely to intercross, uniformity of character is ultimately acquired.' Freely interbreeding flocks of sheep became uniform, most rabbit breeds produced offspring of intermediate colour and it was impossible to maintain the separate colours. Yet Darwin confessed that, in spite of the fact that 'when two commingled breeds exist at first in nearly equal numbers, the whole will sooner or later become blended', there were examples where mingling did not occur. Angora rabbit coat colour (white or black) never seemed to mix; and grey mice and white mice did not have piebald or pale grey offspring but grey or white. Gärtner's yellow and white mullein *Verbascum* were always yellow or white, never cream or mottled; and there were those snapdragons Darwin had grown at Down.

He crossed normal-flower snapdragons with what were called peloric snapdragons. Peloric snapdragons – with atypical symmetrical flowers – appeared as sports from time to time among normal plants. Darwin crossed the pelorics with the normal snapdragons, first with one type as the male parent, then with the other. From two huge beds of seedlings he raised only normal plants – normal, in every respect, even after Darwin's scrutiny. He allowed the hybrids to cross and set seeds. He obtained 127 seedlings: 88 grew into normal snapdragons; 2 were intermediate in form between the grandparents; and 37 were peloric (2.4 : 1) 'having reverted to the structure of the one grandparent'. But this must be an exception to the general rule, he wrote. In the wild, aberrant forms such as peloric snapdragons would be eliminated by natural selection, and not reappear except by chance. Aberrant forms might appear from time to time but the variation on which natural selection was acting was no more 'chance' than selection itself. Both must be caused by the environment.

Two years had passed since Mendel had provided an explanation of such crosses – two years since Mendel had shown in 1866 that particulate inheritance and sexual reproduction were the basis of variation: that characters did not blend; and that parents contributed equally to the offspring. But Darwin did not know of Mendel's explanation of inheritance and, like most of his contemporaries, even if he had known, would not have been ready for it. It would not have provided enough variability. It would not have accounted for the infinitely small gradations between one form and another and it would not have explained the perpetuation of exceptional types in the face of negative selection. And it would not have provided a cause for the first appearance of variations, of sports, like the peloric snap-dragon – or the short-legged Ancona sheep that appeared in Massachusetts one day in 1791 and became the ancestor of a new breed of sheep; or the sudden appearance of a red plum on a tree which, according to Andrew Knight, had borne only yellow plums for forty years.

The laws of inheritance were hidden from Darwin – in the blends and unequal fusions – and all the efforts of natural selection to develop cross-fertilization only led to vigorous offspring and uniformity of character. So where was he to look for the cause of variation? There must be a cause to be discovered. The Darwinian model of evolution could not work unless individuals varied from one to another and so he must find a cause. In the *Origin* he had failed; and seven years later – after seven years of extensive reading and research – he was not much nearer. The search had become 'a passion', he wrote to Huxley, 'to connect all such facts by some sort of hypothesis.'

In 1862, Darwin thought he had found where to look for a

cause of variation. He was regretfully coming to the conclusion
that it was the physical environment that was directly responsible
for it. He was regretful because, in 1862, he found it so
'confoundedly doubtful'. But if geraniums with uniformly
coloured leaves were grown in a new environment, some of them,
it had been reported, developed and perpetuated variegated
leaves. The colours of Hungarian kidney beans could not be
preserved in plants grown in England. 'From the direct action of
a humid climate and poor pasture the horse rapidly decreases
in size in the Falkland Islands.' Yet Darwin freely admitted
that there were exceptions: the peacock and the turkey kept
their original form after years of domestication in a foreign
climate. Thus, the chapter 'Direct and Definite Action of the
External Conditions of Life' – in *Variation* – ended on a doubtful note.

The next chapter looked at the effects of use and disuse.

There was evidence, he decided, that the development of
certain parts of the skeleton of domestic animals had been
modified by the effects of increased or decreased use: the size of
the pigeon's toes, the rudimentary wings of the silkworm. In
contrast, some rudimentary organs appeared suddenly and could
not be accounted for by the accumulation of the effects of disuse.
There was the possibility of correlated variability to account for
that phenomenon. 'We may borrow an illustration from Mr
Herbert Spencer, who remarks that, when the Irish elk acquired
its gigantic horns, weighing above one hundred pounds,
numerous co-ordinated changes of structure would have been
indispensable.'

The laws of variation, according to Darwin, were that
increased use and disuse had probably led to inherited variation;
and variations apparently not connected directly with use or
disuse were due to correlated variability. He formulated an
hypothesis to account for variation. In 1862, quoting the
Cambridge mineralogist William Whewell that 'hypotheses may
often be of service to science, when they involve a certain portion

of incompleteness, and even of error', Darwin ventured to advance 'the hypothesis of Pangenesis'.

Pangenesis was the formation in the cells of minute granules or gemmules which circulated freely in the body, increased by division and assembled by mutual affinity in the reproductive cells. Thus, the gemmules were passed from one generation to the next: sometimes altered in an individual's lifetime, sometimes unchanged. Should any part of an individual be modified by changes in the conditions of existence, the gemmules would 'naturally reproduce the same modification'. It would generally need several generations of exposure to changed conditions for the modification to become innate. Pangenesis explained regeneration: cut off the leg of a salamander and the circulating gemmules would collect at the wound and make a new leg. It explained parthenogenesis, too: the gemmules from all over the body – not just from the reproductive organs – formed the next generation; and it showed that asexual reproduction was little different from sexual. It explained the curious phenomenon of the potato tubers where, it was reported, white and blue tubers joined at an eye gave rise – at that eye – to mottled tubers. (Darwin admitted that his own experiments with potato tubers had failed.) Thus, gemmules – circulating and commingling – were the key to variation: so small that they could go inside an egg or pollen grain, and thoroughly diffuse throughout the body.

Darwin confessed he did not understand how the gemmules assembled in the sex organs.

In crosses between distinctive forms, the gemmules might not be delivered in the same quantity, or have the same potency. Crosses between blue and white pigeons always resulted in blue pigeons. Either the blue parent was contributing more gemmules than the white parent or blue gemmules were stronger than white gemmules. Gemmules could account for inequality of parental contribution and blending inheritance.

When Huxley read the proofs of *Variation*, he pointed out that pangenesis was similar to views expressed by Buffon and Charles

Bonnet in the previous century. Darwin acknowledged them in a long footnote, together with Richard Owen and Herbert Spencer. But forms of pangenesis could be traced back to Hippocrates – cropping up again in the works of Galen – before being taken up by eighteenth-century French biologists. Buffon's 'elaborate system of particles' was based on food: molecules in an organism's food were absorbed by the organs and freed again when the organs were formed in order to make buds or sex elements for transmission to the offspring. Buffon believed that dogs that had their tails cut off, for several generations, transmitted shorter and shorter tails. Pierre Louis Moreau de Maupertuis sought an explanation of the inheritance of polydactyly and opted for a pangenesis theory similar to Darwin's. Owen had a similar idea to account for parthenogenesis and, in 1863, Herbert Spencer came up with 'physiological units'. Spencer's units – like Darwin's gemmules – came from all over the body and found their way to the sex organs. When Darwin discovered Spencer's theory he feared that he might be accused of plagiarism – at first sight, the theories were identical. But, to Darwin's relief, Spencer wrote and said they were not. Spencer maintained that it was the total external and internal environment that affected the units: 'each unit', he argued, 'must be differently affected from any of the rest by aggregate action of the rest upon it.' Thus, only a change in the total organism had value for evolution. Spencer was right: Darwin's pangenesis was different.

There was no mention of Lamarck in *Variation*. Darwin always maintained that he had derived nothing from Lamarck's theory – in spite of having read about it in Lyell's *Principles*, where it was condemned for advocating transmutation of species by gradual change in direct response to the environment. Lamarck's organisms, forced into a new environment, 'changed their habits', then, he claimed, 'the less used organs perish slowly, whilst others that are at an advantage develop more and acquire a vigour and a size proportional to their use.' Moving fluids – interacting with tissues – were affected by the tissue and conveyed its condition to the reproductive organs. The more complex the animal, the more rapid the flow and the quicker the change. Mammals changed faster than fish, fish faster than crustaceans. In Lamarck's theory of the inheritance of acquired characters – as in Darwin's pangenesis – the essential thought was that modifications of the body could affect the germ cells, could change the heritable material of the species.

Darwin was searching for a cause of variation, Lamarck for a cause of evolution. Darwin rejected variation as the directing cause of evolution: selection was the directing cause, acting on the variation between varieties and individuals. Lamarck postulated inherited acquired characters as the directing cause of evolution. The two theories were, in essentials, antagonistic; yet, in the search for a cause of variation, they were compatible. Lamarck's theory was not a precursor of Darwin's theory of evolution – for, as Darwin pointed out, Lamarck would still need selection to complete his theory – but it was a precursor of pangenesis.

Darwin had to put forward an hypothesis for the cause of variation because, he felt, his theory of evolution by natural selection would be incomplete without it. He had been struggling with it for years and, as he wrote to Lyell in 1867, 'pangenesis is 26 or 27 years old.' It had been taking shape before the first draft of the 1844 *Essay*. By the time he was writing it into *Variation*, Darwin was anxious – he admitted it to Hooker – but he had to tie everything together by 'an intelligible thread'. To Asa Gray, he called pangenesis 'a mad dream'; and, after the publication of *Variation*, he wrote again to Hooker: 'I fear pangenesis is stillborn.' But he felt sure it would survive to reappear 'begotten by some other father and christened by some other name.' Darwin still believed it in 1880 by which time, he realized, most people had rejected pangenesis.

Pangenesis had a mixed reception from the start. Lyell was not enthusiastic but admitted he could not stop thinking about it.

Huxley was doubtful but finally rejected it. George Bentham, the botanist, admiring *Variation* for all its useful botanical facts, could not digest pangenesis. The greatest criticism, however, came from the Catholic anatomist St George Mivart. Mivart had greeted the *Origin* with approval but his own *Genesis of Species* (1870) was a complete about-turn. Included in a general attack on Darwinism was a special attack on pangenesis. How could such a thing be true, he argued, when everyone knew that Jews had been circumcised for generations but still had foreskins. Mademoiselle Roger had translated the *Origin* into French and, in 1869, was preparing a third edition. In the introduction she abused pangenesis. Darwin was incensed – pangenesis had no relation to the *Origin* – so he changed his translator.

In the land of Lamarck, pangenesis was not a success but it had a different fate in Germany. Darwinism had swept Germany in the early 1860s and the inheritance of acquired characters became an accepted part of the theory. In fact, Ernst Haeckel believed it to be an indispensable factor in every 'true monistic theory of evolution'. Haeckel modified pangenesis itself to conform to Hermann Helmholtz's philosophy that 'all laws must finally be merged in laws of motion.' Heredity, therefore, was the transfer of motion from one place to another, variation the change in the motion.

The philosophers liked it, the biologists did not. But it was Darwin's cousin Francis Galton who first submitted pangenesis to experiment and delivered a serious blow to it. Galton had started work on heredity in 1865, collecting statistics for a study, 'Hereditary Talent and Character', which was elaborated into his first book on heredity, *Hereditary Genius*, in 1869. He decided that heredity was much more important in determining character than environment. He was less concerned with finding a cause for heredity than in discovering what was inherited; less concerned with heredity in the individual than in how heredity affected the population. At first, he accepted pangenesis but failed to understand how gemmules could work. He decided to look first in the blood. With the help of the official dissector of the London Zoological Society, he devised a method – by joining the carotid arteries – of interchanging the blood of two rabbits; one was silver-grey, the other white. The silver-grey rabbit, with the white rabbit's blood, produced silver-grey offspring and the white rabbit, with the silver-grey rabbit's blood, produced white offspring. Galton concluded that pangenesis was wrong and that it was more likely that heritable characters were to be found in the solid structure of the reproductive organs. Darwin was not amused and wrote to *Nature* denouncing Galton's conclusions. He claimed that the gemmules were not necessarily in the blood but 'diffused through the body'. Galton agreed to continue his experiments for another two years in close consultation with Darwin. No further results were published. Galton rejected pangenesis – 'nature prevails enormously over nurture' – and, in later editions of *Variation*, Darwin added a footnote admitting that gemmules might be carried in the blood – but not necessarily.

Galton was approaching the problem from a totally different angle from Darwin. Already, in 1865, what has become known as his law of ancestral inheritance had been clearly stated: a man received half his inheritance from his father, one quarter from his grandfather, one eighth from each great-grandparent – 'the share decreasing step by step, in a geometrical ratio, with great rapidity.' Galton was being directed by his statistics to observe that parents contributed equally to the offspring.

By 1889, blending inheritance too was looking less sound, although Galton believed that some characters – like stature – showed evidence of it: eye colour did not blend, otherwise Englishmen would all have hazel eyes. Despite such inconsistency, he did not totally reject blending inheritance and, as a result, failed to arrive at a complete understanding of heredity. But Galton applied his statistics to demography: he tried to describe the distribution and inheritance of characters in populations; he was less interested in how such characters might be passed to the individual. It was the individual inheritance and variation that interested Darwin.

When Wallace read *Variation* he accepted pangenesis for want of a better cause of inherited variation. But he was interested in the problem of sterility between allied species which Darwin raised in a chapter on hybridism. Darwin did not believe that degrees of sterility between allied species could evolve gradually: any sterility, he argued, would be selected against. Wallace argued, in contrast, that two populations of a species, each adapted to slightly different conditions, would be favoured by even slight barriers to crossing. Sterility, in fact, could be selected for. Although Darwin disagreed on grounds that sterility could not be selected for – those that failed to leave offspring were selected against – he had provided an example of speciation in the *Origin* where a continuous population differed at the two ends of its range. The intermediates were the less well adapted and decreased in number and finally disappeared, leaving the two extremes – the two ends of the range – to become separate species. Mainly, Darwin thought, species diverged when they were separated spatially, by changes in land formation or by dispersal.

Pangenesis soon dropped from the correspondence between Darwin and Wallace. Wallace took the view that he would accept the theory until something better turned up. That something better did not appear until after Darwin's death.

The accumulating evidence of the German cytologists – like the statistical work of Galton – had been casting doubt on both the inequality theory of parental contributions to offspring and blending inheritance. When chromosomes were discovered in 1876 both propositions became untenable. Chromosomes might mix and even be selected during the development of the individual but they were discrete bodies carried from one generation to the next in the nucleus of the sex cells and they appeared to retain their identity. With the ideas of inequality and blending rejected, the next blow to Darwin's laws of inheritance came in 1885 from the work of August Weismann, Professor of Zoology at Freiburg in Germany. Weismann declared that – from his study of insects – it was clear that the reproductive cells of animals were distinct, identifiable and differentiated at an early stage in development in both males and females. There was no way in which the body cells could affect the germ cells. The germ cells – or, more specifically, the nucleus of the germ cells – were independent of the body, to the extent that the germ cells formed the body only as a means of transmission to the next generation. Thus, the germ cells were continuous from generation to generation and the body cells were not. If Weismann's theory was acceptable, then pangenesis and Lamarckism was finished. Wallace accepted Weismannism immediately but others were still wavering when the British Association for the Advancement of Science met in Manchester in 1887. 'The Transmission of Acquired Characters' was debated in the presence of Weismann. Two years later, there was a long correspondence in *Nature* entitled 'Lamarck versus Weismann'.

Herbert Spencer was worried that, if it could be proved that acquired characters were not inherited, his whole philosophy would be undermined. He could not accept small innate variations as the material on which selection acted. Spencer's philosophy required big jumps – the jumps of a well adapted animal whose total adaptation to the environment had been inherited through the total adaptation of the physiological units. Alteration of a part – a single organ – could not succeed because it would disrupt the 'harmony of the whole'. Spencer believed in Cuvierian co-ordination of parts from which both Darwin and Wallace had more or less disentangled themselves. Gradualism – and gradualism on a tiny scale directed by natural selection – was the stuff of evolution, whether such variation was due to gemmules or chromosomes.

Pangenesis lapsed in Darwin's lifetime but he never gave up his belief in the inheritance of acquired characters even if, as he regretted, he might have been mistaken over the mechanism: in

1880, he could still write that 'habitual movements are inherited by plants.'

The final blow, or so it seemed – to pangenesis, inheritance of acquired characters, inequality of parental contribution and blending inheritance – occurred in 1900 when Mendelian and de Vriesian theories of inheritance reached the scientific world.

5. The Descent of Man

'I might have adduced for this same purpose the differences between the races of man, which are so strongly marked: I may add that some little light can apparently be thrown on the origin of these differences chiefly through sexual selection of a particular kind, but without here entering on copious details any reasoning would appear frivolous,' Darwin 1859.

By the time *Variation* was published in 1868, Darwin was collecting material for another major work, one that was to have a better future than *Variation*.

In the *Origin*, Darwin had said little about the origin of man except to hint that sexual selection might be important in the evolution of racial differences and to recognize that 'light will be thrown on the origin of man and his history'. But it was man's position in the world that interested his readers. The consequences for man – of Darwin's hypothesis – were clear. Man was no longer at the centre of the living world, a created being. He was not the product of a Divine Plan – evolution had no plan. No matter how tactful the author, Darwin's *Origin* shattered nineteenth-century man's belief in his traditional role.

It was Huxley, however, who first championed the cause of the natural evolution of man. He had been provoked in 1860 at the Oxford meeting of the British Association for the Advancement of Science. Samuel Wilberforce the Bishop of Oxford – primed by Richard Owen who had earlier asserted that man's brain differed more from the gorilla's than the gorilla's from the lowest monkey's – launched an attack on the Darwinian theory and, it is alleged, asked Huxley whether he was descended from an ape through his grandfather or his grandmother. The unphilosophical nature of Darwin's theory or its elements of alleged fantasy might be a basis for serious discussion, not for personal insults.

Huxley was provoked to a biting reply. The actual proceedings of the meeting were not recorded and the reply was repeated in several versions. The gist was that Huxley said he would rather be descended from an ape than a bishop who misused his talent, 'whereupon there was unextinguishable laughter among the people, and they listened to the rest of the argument with the greatest attention.' Huxley was followed at the meeting by Hooker with a long pro-Darwinian speech which 'hit him [the Bishop] in the wind at the first shot'. Darwin had a headache and was not present.

Satirists had a field day, caricature and light verse appeared everywhere:

> Eggs were laid as before, but each time more and more
> varieties struggled and bred
> Till one end of the scale dropped its ancestor's tail
> and the other got rid of its head.
> From the bill, in brief words, were developed the Birds,
> unless our tame pigeons and ducks lie;
> From the tail and hind legs, in the second laid eggs,
> the apes and Professor Huxley!

Two years later, the British Association met in Cambridge where Owen attacked Darwin's theory directly: this time, on account of a study he had made of a lemur which, Owen declared, was totally different from man. At that meeting it was a cleric who applauded the theory. The Reverend W. N. Molesworth, unlike Wilberforce, welcomed it as a stimulus to investigation of the Creator's works. After that, the British Association's discussions about man's place in nature took on a more moderate tone.

Meanwhile, Huxley had replied to Owen in print arguing, from anatomical observations, that the feature claimed by Owen to be unique in man – the brain's hippocampus minor (associated with memory) – was not peculiar to man, as it occurred in apes. The hippocampus minor was almost as popular as Huxley's grandparents and reached its zenith in *The Water Babies* by the

Queen's Chaplain, Charles Kingsley. 'Nothing is to be depended on but the great hippopotamus test. If you have a hippopotamus major in your brain, you are no ape, though you have four hands, no feet and were more apish than the apes of all aperies. But, if a hippopotamus major is discovered in one single ape's brain, nothing will save your great-great-great-great-great-great-great-great-great-great-greatest grandmother from having been an ape too.'

In 1863 *Man's Place in Nature* by Huxley and *The Antiquity of Man* by Lyell were published in London. Lyell was not yet ready to accept evolution of the living world – despite his evolutionary geology – but he had to admit that recent fossil finds of human bones needed an explanation. *The Antiquity of Man* was mainly a description of those finds. The 1847 discovery of ancient flint implements near Abbeville and part of a skull in Gibraltar and the 1857 discovery of the Neanderthal skull near Düsseldorf compelled the attention of Britain's leading geologist.

There could be no question of the antiquity of the objects and there was no doubt that Neanderthal man was different – but not that different – from modern man. It looked like an example of evolutionary change. Lyell described the finds faithfully but, with 'ifs' and 'buts', wriggled out of the obvious conclusion. It was, he explained, a 'pre-concerted arrangement' which 'presents us with a picture of the ever-increasing dominion of mind over matter.'

Huxley made no concessions to creation. Anatomical features, embryonic stages, fossil remains all combined to show, according to Huxley, that man was a mammal like a dog or a monkey but most like a gorilla. The question of man's superior brain was answered with a mass of anatomical data: there was nothing about the human brain – except its size – that made it different from a gorilla's. *Man's Place in Nature* was written to establish by comparative anatomy that man was part of the natural order and had evolved like other animals from animal ancestors: 'if any process of physical causation can be discovered by which genera and families of ordinary animals have been produced, that process of causation is amply sufficient to account for the origin of man.' That process was Darwin's theory of evolution by natural selection but, when Huxley considered it, gradual change was not always apparent. 'Remember if you will', he wrote, 'that there is no existing link between man and the gorilla.' Perhaps man – with that gap – was uniquely created after all? But 'do not forget that there is a no less strong line of demarcation,' Huxley reasoned, 'between the Gorilla and the Orang.' Man and the gorilla might be separate creations but Huxley opted for a jerky Darwinian evolution.

In the following year, Wallace wrote an article for the *Anthropological Review* in which he argued that natural selection could account for the evolution of man. He argued that man's physical evolution took place before his mental evolution. Upright carriage had come before enlargement of the brain and reduction in the teeth. As early man ranged farther away from his ancestral home in Africa to colder climates – new food resources and new competitors – useful variations in his behaviour occurred. Tool-making became an asset and was selected for, like language. Trade and communication developed.

What was Darwin doing while his followers were discussing the origin of man? In June 1860, he was suffering from one of his headaches. But Darwin was keeping track of the discussions: 'I am astonished at your success and audacity,' he wrote to Hooker, 'I had no idea you had this power.' He expressed deep interest in *The Antiquity of Man* but criticized Lyell for not having 'spoken fairly out what he thought about the derivation of species.' He chided him for not making public what he admitted in private: that he had 'given up belief in the immutability of specific forms.' He praised Huxley's *Man's Place in Nature*: 'how splendid some pages are . . . but I fear the book will not be popular.' He deplored the reviewer for the *Athenaeum*, who denounced Huxley for degrading man and Lyell for making him old. He was delighted by Wallace's article in the *Anthropological Review*: 'the great leading idea is quite new to me viz that during late ages the mind will have been modified more than the body.' At the end of the letter, Darwin offered Wallace his notes on man but Wallace refused them. Later, Wallace's views on man changed: he found it necessary to invent a spiritual force to guide the evolution of man. Darwin groaned but, by 1869, he was immersed in 'a little essay on the origin of mankind'.

The 'little essay' would consider whether man had evolved from some pre-existing form, how it could have come about; and it would compare the present races of man. It was to be a development of a sentence in the *Origin* that asserted that the races of man had evolved through sexual selection.

In the *Origin*, a short section explained the general principles of sexual selection. Sexual selection depended on two different intraspecific activities: the male struggle with male for possession of females; and female choice of mate. As Darwin assembled his evidence, the subject seemed to have more and more general application in the animal world. The evidence accumulated in the usual way – Darwin never left anything out – and so the 'little essay' grew to 700 pages: *The Descent of Man*, published in 1871.

In the *Origin*, Darwin had given examples of sexual selection: the bellowing male alligators; the aggressive male stag beetles; the male displays of the Guiana rock-thrushes; and the magnificent displays of birds of paradise. As he assembled facts for *The Descent of Man*, he came to the conclusion that his new theory of sexual selection could account for most of the colour in the animal world.

Wallace believed that colour could be accounted for by natural selection. It provided recognition between male and female, between parent and offspring, between individuals of the same species. It acted as a signal to warn off predators. The drab colours of female birds, Wallace believed, could be accounted for as camouflage to protect them sitting on the nest. Darwin preferred sexual selection as an explanation of colour although he was, as he admitted to Wallace, 'undergoing severe distress about protection and sexual selection.' By 1877, Darwin had diverged so far from Wallace that further discussion was useless. 'You will not be surprised,' he wrote to Wallace, 'that I differ altogether from you about sexual colours.'

More than half *The Descent of Man* was about colour in animals, other than man. Darwin had collected examples from jellyfish to mammals and they were all included whether they were examples of sexual selection or not. The transparent jellyfish was concealed from predators, the bright sponge a warning to predators. It was difficult, he admitted, to account for the bright colours of worms but it seemed unlikely that female worms would exert choice in pairing or male worms 'struggle together in rivalry'. The bright colours of male crustaceans, however, were surely developed because they attracted or excited females. Among the invertebrates, butterflies provided the most striking examples of colour dimorphism and evidence for Darwin's theory. 'It is impossible to admit,' he wrote, 'that the brilliant colours of butterflies and of some few moths, have commonly been acquired for the sake of protection – hence I am led to believe that the females prefer or are most excited by the most brilliant males.' After butterflies, birds. Darwin filled his pages with colour and song – from the song of the linnet to the feathers of the Argus pheasant. And the bright songs and the plumage gave as much pleasure to the males as to the females. For did not birds sing long after courtship and the sparrow learn the superior song of the linnet? Did not the waving plumes of the male birds of paradise excite the whole flock by their splendour? And did not the female Argus pheasant choose the most beautiful male by the fine markings of his feathers? 'As any fleeting fashion in dress comes to be admired by man, so with birds a change of almost any kind in structure or colouring of the feathers in the male appears to have been admired by the female.' No wonder Wallace criticized Darwin for his 'anthropomorphic' theory of female choice. But Darwin went further – with examples from domestic animals – when he drew an analogy between pigeon fanciers and female choice.

Due respect was paid to Wallace's rule, that birds with concealed nests were, both male and female, usually bright coloured. But the end result of Darwin's analysis was that 'bright and conspicuous colours have generally been acquired by the males through variation and sexual selection.' He was reluctant to accept Wallace's proposition that natural selection acted differentially on male and female though he accepted it as an explanation of the female barnacle with the tiny complemental males. The elaborate colours of butterflies, beetles and vertebrates could not be accounted for by differential selection: that produced, for example, camouflaged females and bright males. Not even dull offspring were the necessary product of differential selection because the colour of young birds was found to follow strict rules. The offspring were as dull as the duller of the parents: and if both parents were dull, the offspring were dull; and if both parents were bright, the offspring were bright; and if the parents' had a summer and a winter plumage, the offspring wore the winter plumage. The young and the females were the ancestral forms and the males had diverged through female choice and male rivalry. Darwin, as usual, looked for a single cause to explain all the facts. It was neater and more philosophical.

There was, too, the complicating consideration of inheritance which had never seriously worried Wallace. Darwin was still worrying over the causes of variation and now he was faced with the equally baffling problem of differential inheritance. Some characters, like the pollen baskets of honey bees, were found in both sexes even though they were not used by males; others, like the brilliant blue wings of the male Indian blue butterfly *Lycaena oegon*, were confined to one sex. How was it possible for characters to be transmitted through both sexes and yet regularly appear only in one? Pangenesis came to the rescue once again. The gemmules circulated in both male and female but, through the action of natural or artificial selection, they were only allowed to manifest themselves in one and were suppressed in the other.

The final problem was how females could exert a choice unless outnumbered by the males. Polygamous species were easy: the most beautiful male was chosen by the most females. Presumably with equal numbers and monogamy all found mates regardless. There were no records of relative numbers of male and female butterflies or birds but Darwin reckoned they were probably about equal, like the 99.7 male to 100 female racehorse foals; or, exceptionally, the 110 male to 100 female greyhound pups. Darwin invented an ingenious solution: females that matured early got first choice of the most beautiful mate; thus, they bred early and left more offspring than females maturing late.

Female choice seemed to account for the colours of wings but did it account for sexual differences like male antlers, manes and the male's greater size? Darwin described the horns of antelope locking together as the males kneeled in conflict, the huge size and aggressive behaviour of male seals, the odours emitted by musk deer and the bright-coloured face of mandrills. He confessed ignorance of the role of female choice in those cases but, from observations of domestic animals, he concluded that it existed. More important, however, was the 'law of battle' for possession of females. Yet horns and antlers were not only used in male rivalry but also in defence, so it seemed strange to him that females were without them. Darwin concluded that the anomaly could be accounted for only by the 'form of inheritance which has prevailed'.

But what had all this to do with man, ostensibly the subject of the book? In the first part of *The Descent of Man* Darwin described the evolution of man through natural selection. First of all, he had to argue his case for the close affinity of man with apes and monkeys: such as a common susceptibility to similar diseases and parasites; a similar embryonic development – as von Baer and Huxley had noticed – and the possession of rudimentary organs, like the muscles of the ear, which no longer served a purpose. Having established the animal nature of man, he went on to discuss the other ingredients of his general theory.

Everyone knew that individuals varied one from another but there was again that nagging problem of inheritance. In man, it was the same as in other animals: the conditions of existence caused changes and the acquired information was carried by the gemmules to the reproductive organs. Use and disuse were clearly important, for were not watchmakers short-sighted, and was not short-sightedness inherited? For selection to pick particular variants there must be plenty to choose from. There were certainly plenty of children in the world: the population of the USA had doubled in twenty-four years and even savages, as Malthus remarked, produced more than enough offspring to maintain the size of the population. All the Malthusian checks must have been at work on human populations that had remained stable in the past: starvation, disease, late marriage, abortion and infanticide. That was natural selection.

Man was variable, man reproduced more of his kind than was required for a stable population; therefore, selection in the past had been responsible for the evolution of man. 'Barbarous' man came first, civilized man was a later evolutionary development. He had seen the 'poor tormented wretches' of Tierra del Fuego and 'it was difficult to believe they are fellow creatures and inhabitants of the same world.' They must be barbarous; nineteenth-century man, civilized. (Victorian England was the best of all possible worlds and its inhabitants at the highest point of evolution.)

Basing his judgement on examples accumulated from anthropologists like J. C. Prichard and E. B. Tylor, Darwin concluded that most of the differences between races could not be correlated with any aspect of the environment. The major influence on the evolution of man was sexual selection, not natural selection.

He enumerated the different sexual characters of the human male and female. Men were taller, heavier and stronger than women; men had more prominent eyebrows, more hair and a deeper voice; they were more courageous, aggressive and energetic; and they were more inventive. In contrast, women were rounder, matured earlier and had a broader pelvis; they were imitative, perceptive, intuitive and less selfish than men. The chief difference between men and women, however, lay in their intellectual power, 'man attaining to a higher eminence, in whatever he takes up, than can woman – whether requiring deep thought, reason or imagination or merely the uses of the senses and hands.' Those striking differences, Darwin argued, could not have been the result of use and disuse, of the inheritance of acquired characters; for hard work and the development of muscles was not the prerogative of man: 'in barbarian societies women work as hard or harder.' In any case, the intellectual powers in man were normally developed before the reproductive age and their heritable component would not be affected by the environment. Intellectual superiority of the human male was innate but how had it come about? By sexual selection, said Darwin, not by female choice. Man's beard might be the result of female choice and, in some tribes, a certain kind of beauty might be attributed to it; but, considering the condition of women in barbarous tribes – where men kept women 'in a far more abject state of bondage than does the male of any animal' – it was probably the male that chose. Different standards of beauty selected by the male might, thus, account for some of the differentiation of tribes.

The sexual selection that operated in the human species was the type found to be widespread among mammals: the struggle between males for possession of the most females. Man competed to become the best warrior, the best hunter, in order to have the greatest number of wives. He exercised his wits to protect his family from other men. Thus, intelligence and muscular power were inherited to a greater extent by males than females.

The Descent of Man ended with a conclusion that Darwin recognized would be 'highly distasteful to many'. A conclusion that man had lowly origins, that he was descended from barbarians – even modern man with 'his god-like intellect'.

The Descent of Man was received with caution. Nevertheless, 7500 copies were sold in 1871 and, as Huxley remarked, it was very popular with the ladies. Reviews were not abusive, at worst contentious, which Darwin took as proof of the increasing liberality of England. The *Athenaeum* was contemptuous: 'no man will ever develop religion out of a dog or christianity out of a cat.' The *Edinburgh Review* criticized Darwin for his lack of logical power and sound philosophy but praised him for his ingenuity. *The Times* came nearest to abuse: *The Descent* was the sort of loose philosophy and morality that was contributing to the disorganization of France; it was disgraceful that a man with a reputation like Darwin should advance such reckless views on such flimsy evidence. The Catholic biologist Mivart returned to his attack in the *Quarterly Review*. Mivart accepted that the physical part of man had evolved from animals but, like Wallace, he insisted that some spiritual force – in his case God – had created man's soul. The soul distinguished man from the rest of the living world. He accused Darwin of being a mere collector of facts with a power of reasoning in inverse ratio to his power of observation. He demanded proof of man's evolution through sexual selection and concluded that Darwin exaggerated its efficacy just as he had exaggerated survival of the fittest in the *Origin*. Darwin never forgave Mivart – referring to him as a 'pettifogger' and 'Old Bailey lawyer' – and supposed 'that accursed religious bigotry is at the root of it.' Wallace was worried about Darwin's interpretation of inheritance and could not see how any form of sexual selection through female choice could operate: for 'women are more or less a matter of purchase.' Later, he came to regard female choice as the directing evolutionary force of social progress.

Huxley found himself in difficulty over man's social evolution. How could natural selection have produced organized societies if it favoured male aggressiveness and self-assertion? Darwin had tried to answer this by arguing that tribes or societies would be selected against other tribes for their average qualities. But 'living together', wrote Huxley, 'is contrary to the struggle for existence in nature.' There must be some other explanation for the apparent persistence of social man for it was inconceivable that it was not a stable state. He opted for a form of social evolution: social bonds might lower the fitness of an individual but increase the chances of the tribe. Education would raise the social level though it would not contribute to the physical inheritance of the individual. Huxley did not believe in the inheritance of acquired characters but he believed passionately in the need for universal education.

Darwin's male contemporaries were more flattered by female choice than male rivalry and ready to apply it with enthusiasm. Who did not want to be the chosen male? Galton was wholehearted in his support. What better explanation of female coyness, he asked, than sexual selection? Coyness must be an 'essential condition' of sexual selection: woman must not accept the firstcomer but wait and see what else might turn up before making her choice.

In Germany, *The Descent of Man* was a tremendous success. Haeckel accepted that males chose the handsomest females in some animals; in others, females chose the handsomest males. In this way, special features and secondary sexual characters would be accentuated. With the inheritance of acquired characters, differences would increase rapidly; and, therefore, 'the rise of the human race' would be 'due for the most part to the advanced sexual selection which our ancestors exercised in choosing their mates.' Furthermore – though Haeckel did not explain exactly how it would work – 'it is to sexual selection that we owe family life, which is the chief foundation of civilisation.' Even Weismann thought the principle of sexual selection was 'incontestable' and the German naturalist Fritz Müller was completely won over.

Thus, the origin of man by natural law which, by the 1870s,

was taken for granted in most circles, was made more palatable by Darwinian concepts of male superiority and female choice. It was delightful, in fact, if the appreciation of beauty and intelligence were a key to survival. Darwin was pleased that *The Descent of Man* was popular but he was disappointed that so few naturalists were enthusiastic about sexual selection.

By the 1890s, attitudes had changed and the majority of biologists seemed to have accepted sexual selection. The seal of respectability was set on it with the review of Wallace's *Darwinism* by Ray Lankester in 1889 and the publication of *The Colours of Animals* by E. B. Poulton in 1890. Wallace summarized all his ideas on colour in *Darwinism* and concluded that there were many selective factors responsible for its evolution. He had never denied the importance of male rivalry but, in most cases, Darwin's female choice was not applicable. Lankester did not agree with Wallace and rejected his case against female choice.

In Poulton's great summary of the meaning of colour Darwin's theory was triumphant. Poulton accepted Wallace's recognition and warning colours but was more enthusiastic about sexual selection, partly because it endowed animals with an aesthetic sense. Any bright colour would do for recognition but only beauty would succeed where an active choice had to be made. The idea was comforting for those who saw only the random cruelty of natural selection. Man had evolved from animals through the appreciation of beauty; and animals with an aesthetic sense were acceptable ancestors.

Two days later – when the last page proofs of *The Descent of Man* went back to the publisher – Darwin started *The Expression of the Emotions in Man and Animals* (1872) to give further support to the argument that man resembled other animals. Man was not losing but animals were gaining qualities they had not been suspected of having – except, of course, souls. *Expression of the Emotions* was the outcome of an interest in man's behaviour that went back to his encounters with the natives of Tierra del Fuego, during the *Beagle* voyage; and continued with observations of his own children, aided by his reading of Charles Bell's *Anatomy and Philosophy of Expression* (1806).

Darwin was clearly considering the evolution of man at an early stage in his thoughts on species, for he had opened his first notebook on man in 1838. If man were unique – because of his language, morals, intellect and soul – it would be essential to show that those characters had evolved through selection. 'He who understands baboon,' he entered in his notebook, 'would do more toward metaphysics than Locke.' There were entries on the wide range of emotions in dogs, the similarity of those emotions to emotions in man: 'hyaena pisses from fear so does man – and so does dog.' He collected information at irregular intervals – with occasional jottings in the man notebooks – until 1867 when he decided to be more systematic. He devised a questionnaire for · physiologists and sent it to men who lived among 'savages'.

There was no reference to the incubating *Expression of the Emotions* in the *Origin*: man was not to be the subject of the first announcement of evolutionary theory; but a comparison of man's mental powers with the powers of lower animals – and of one tribe with another – occupied three chapters of *The Descent of Man*. While admitting that there was an immense difference in the intellectual powers of man and apes, Darwin nevertheless decided that the difference was one of degree: social instincts and moral qualities, he decided, had been acquired with the development of the brain – there was no mind-body problem for Darwin – through the inheritance of acquired characters and male rivalry. It was, of course, this sort of argument that brought down on his head the wrath of critics like Mivart.

Not all the material he had collected over the years could be incorporated in *The Descent of Man* and, as nothing was ever wasted, the leftovers turned into a new book.

He identified facial expressions that were similar in man and other animals, and man's facial expressions that were common to all tribes. His first concern was to put some sort of order into the mound of information. He classified his data according to three rules. First there were habits, such as the acquired habit of unnatural gaits in trained horses. The habitual practice of a learned gait, mediated by the nervous system, facilitated its performance and eventually it became an inherited character of horses. Thus, there were habits inherited from distant ancestors, like sneering, which might be related to the aggressive exposure of the canine teeth in baboons. Second, there was the law of antithesis: a cat advanced aggressively, low on the ground, with its tail horizontal; but it curled and purred round its owner's leg with an opposite gesture, with its tail off the ground, vertical. Antithetic activities (the smile was an antithesis of misery) facilitated the same muscles and the same parts of the nervous system and were duly inherited. Third, there was the law of direct action of the nervous system. Fear, for example, was expressed by actions which would occur in the actual need-for-flight situation: like trembling, palpitations and pallor. All classes of emotion, he decided, could be interpreted as evolutionary events. There was no need to suppose, as Bell had done, that human facial muscles were a special provision for the expression of human emotions but rather follow Spencer and interpret expressions as a form of nervous activity which originally accompanied an action. Aggressive expressions, according to Spencer, were the original accompaniment of killing. More difficult to account for were expressions like blushing which, for Bell, was an expression designed by the Creator so that the inner soul could reveal itself, and, for the Frenchman Gratiolet, was a sign of man's perfection. Darwin had already considered blushing in 1839 and had interpreted it as a rush of blood to a part of the body that was being given special attention, either because the part was being looked at by someone else or because the blusher thought the part was being looked at. There must, Darwin thought, be a physiological explanation of all emotions.

The Expression of the Emotions was full of examples, mainly anecdotal; but it served to show that even the emotions and other intellectual qualities of man could be traced in lower animals. There was no reason to suppose that something special was required to give man those qualities. Such evolution showed that mental and moral qualities could be regarded as dependent directly on the brain. There was no soul except insofar as it represented the interplay of nervous reactions. Expressions could be acquired like anything else by habit and inheritance. The inheritance of acquired characters was an essential part of the theory. There was, however, no mention of sexual selection in *The Expression of the Emotions*, no differentiation of man from woman.

The *Edinburgh Review* was scathing: the amusing stories and grotesque illustrations, it claimed, showed a marked falling-off in philosophical and scientific interest because of the author's one-sided devotion to a single interpretation of all phenomena.

Was Darwin becoming boring with his endless examples and his single theory? *The Expression of the Emotions* sold 5267 copies on the day of publication.

And there were still some scraps left. Articles on inherited instinct, the habits of ants, perception in the lower animals and a biographical sketch of an infant – his first son born thirty-seven years earlier – were published. With the publication of the last scrap in 1877, the subject of man was closed.

6. Plant Movement

'I cannot doubt that the continued selection of slight variations, either in the leaves, flowers, or the fruit, will produce races differing from each other chiefly in these characters,' Darwin 1859.

In 1833, Darwin was walking on the shores of Tierra del Fuego, between the trees and the snow-capped mountains. Small flowers carpeted a band of peat and among them was a sundew. On the heath on the fringes of Ashdown Forest – twenty-seven years later – when he was already at work on *Variation* – a sundew attracted his attention again. It attracted his attention because of the insects trapped on its leaves. He had heard that plants caught insects – Linnaeus had mentioned the Venus flytrap – but it was the first time he had seen it happening. Being the inquisitive naturalist he was, he brought some sundews home from his holiday and gave them insects. Why should a plant trap insects? What was the cause? Nothing was without a cause. Darwin was fascinated: 'I care more about *Drosera* [sundew] than the origin of all the species in the world,' he wrote to Lyell at the end of 1860. He was launched into an investigation of insectivorous plants which was to be ready for publication in 1875.

The *Drosera* work continued in parallel with the investigations on the fertilization of orchids, on cross-fertilization and the assembling of evidence for *Variation*.

The common sundew *D. rotundifolia* was offered insects and liquids of various blends, tickled and its reactions noted. The leaf's tentacles and glands reacted to pressure and to any liquid containing nitrogenous material. The tentacles curled inwards and the glands oozed a viscid fluid. It was a fascinating phenomenon: a plant that moved in response to external stimulus and that secreted a fluid that trapped insects. Was it possible, he asked – as Dr Curtis of North Carolina had suggested – that the sundew was actually consuming insects? Darwin performed experiment after experiment until he found that leaves put in a solution of glycerine and weak hydrochloric acid could reduce the size of albumen cubes. In a footnote, he assured the reader that albumen was not reduced in control experiments, without leaves. The sundew seemed capable of digesting animal matter: it 'had not been known to exist among plants before'.

Pursuing his usual systematic method, he compared *D. rotundifolia* with six other *Drosera* species, one sent to him by Hooker from the Cape of Good Hope, another from North America and two from Australasia. They seemed much alike and Darwin concluded that all of them probably consumed insects. He could arrange them in a sequence to represent a smooth transition, or evolution, from forms with long leaves, through oblong leaves to forms with round leaves. The Portuguese *Drosophyllum, Bondula* and *Byblus* were similar to *Drosera* but the tentacles and leaves had no power of movement. Perhaps they were ancestral forms – evidence of gradual evolution was everywhere. Then there were the Venus flytrap and the aquatic *Aldrovanda* that could snap their leaves shut to catch an animal. And there were bladderworts that could not digest insects but absorbed the products of their decay. There were other variations: the bird's nest orchid absorbed decaying plant products; and parasites like mistletoe absorbed the products of living plants. Whatever the adaptations, however, they still obtained their carbon from the atmosphere like other plants. But the insectivorous plants lived in nitrogen-poor conditions: in bogs, bare mountains or in pools. Thus, by eating insects, the plants actually supplemented their nitrogen supply. What a wonderful adaptation to the conditions of existence! Might it not be worth looking at less obvious plants for similar adaptations? At the geranium or at the sticky leaves of the saxifrage? Darwin said it all in *Insectivorous Plants* (1875) and no one challenged him until the twentieth century when his results were confirmed and extended at Pavia University.

A plant's ability to digest insects was exciting, but it was the observation on movement that provided stimulus for an extensive series of experiments. Asa Gray had written about cucumber tendrils in 1858 but no one else seemed to have noticed that plants moved; and, certainly, no one had investigated the evolutionary or the functional reasons for movement; and certainly not the cause.

In 1862, the heated greenhouse at Down was completed and Darwin sowed seeds of wild cucumber sent to him by Asa Gray and, soon after, his first observations on climbing plants were reported to Hooker. The stem between the two uppermost leaves – but not the growing tip – was twisting and untwisting. The climbing mechanisms of other plants were recorded. A classification was made. There were plants whose stems twisted spirally round a support, like convolvulus and hops; others that anchored by curling petioles, like clematis; or by tendrils, like the pea. There were plants that used hooks for climbing, like the rose; and plants that climbed by rootlet adhesion, like ivy. The movements were modifications of an irregular sweeping movement – or circumnutation – common to all plants.

The Movements and Habits of Climbing Plants was published as a paper in the *Journal of the Linnean Society* in 1865; and, as a book, in 1875. Darwin did not claim originality for the paper because he knew that others had already commented on plant movement. Plants, he argued, climbed to reach the light and the stimulus was so great that plants, totally unrelated to one another, had acquired similar methods of climbing. Within groups of related plants, twiners had probably evolved into leaf-climbers; and leaf-climbers into tendril-climbers. Twiners were common in tropical forests. Leaf-climbers, with their firmer fixing, might be more typical of windy places. A tendril was an economical version of a leaf. Another satisfactory illustration of gradual evolution had been worked out: with striking examples of the use of homologous organs for different functions; and equally striking examples of similarity of adaptation in unrelated forms, where the conditions of existence were similar. But 'if we imagine how a petiole or branch or flower peduncle first became sensitive to a touch, and acquired the power of bending towards the touched side, we get no answer.'

In his sundew experiments, Darwin became aware of what he called irritability. Glands sent a stimulus to the tentacles, the tentacles bent and sent a stimulus back to the glands. Darwin called it reflex action but admitted it was different from reflex action in animals. By experiment, he convinced himself that the stimulus for reflex action was not travelling in the obvious way, through the vascular bundles. It spread, gradually, from cell to cell. Under the microscope, he saw a purple substance move through the cells from the glands. The nature of the substance eluded him. But whatever the substance that provided the stimulus, the tentacles bent and the phenomenon was worth investigating.

Plant movement had been generally attributed to differential growth but a new theory suggested that water movement through the cells was the primary cause. Darwin thought it more likely to be due to cell contraction and elasticity.

In the summer of 1877, after the publication of *The Different Forms of Flowers*, work was begun with his son Francis on the cause of plant movement. In Germany, botanists had come to the conclusion that the movement was the direct physico-chemical result of the stimulus: light on the cell wall caused it to thicken and contract, bringing the stem towards the stimulus; or light caused stem movement by its direct effect on water content; or light directly stimulated cell growth. But Francis Darwin had worked with Julius Sachs in Germany and shown that roots, contrary to the general opinion, could grow in the light as well as the dark, though more slowly in the light. Simple direct action was not a convincing interpretation.

Charles and Francis investigated. Light directed on to a broad-bean shoot caused it to bend towards the light but if the tip was covered the shoot did not bend. Some substance in the apex of the shoot was being activated by the light and diffused to other parts of the plant that it might bend. Without tip stimulation the substance was not diffused. The resultant movement was not the direct effect of light – any more than tickling a sundew – but mediated through a diffusible substance. The German botanists were wrong about simple direct action. But were they wrong about differential growth as the means of movement? Differential growth, however, passed Darwin's tests and Charles and Francis were able to confirm the theory of their German colleagues.

Darwin investigated sleep in plants, the drooping lupin leaves at night; and found that depression and elevation of the leaf depended on the amount of water in a few cells at the base of its stalk. But what was the adaptive significance? It protected the plant from heat loss: the rapid radiation of heat from its leaves into the cold night air – an hypothesis confirmed after a cold night, by the sad spectacle of the dead plants of an experiment.

Darwin formulated his hypothesis. Heliotropism 'sun turning' and geotropism 'earth turning' – and all other plant movements – could be interpreted as modified circumnutations, effected by the movement of substances through the tissues. The shoot tip and the root tip held the key. *The Power of Movement in Plants* was published in 1880 by Charles Darwin 'assisted by Francis Darwin'.

Thistleton-Dyer, in 1882, summed up Darwin's achievement: 'no one can doubt the importance of what Mr Darwin has done in showing that for the future the phenomenon of plant movement can and indeed must be studied from a single point of view.'

Once again, Darwin had succeeded in assembling and unifying a heap of facts. But circumnutation was not to be the unifying hypothesis for long. Francis Darwin soon rejected it.

Sachs was contemptuous: he despised the simple experimental techniques. But Darwin had almost hit on the physico-chemical explanation of plant movement – plant hormones.

The main Darwinian theme was not absent from the work.

Drooping at night and heliotropism varied in efficiency from plant to plant. There was variation, and variation was inherited. 'We have good reason to believe that habitual movements are inherited by plants.' It was, said Darwin, 'a necessary contingent for this process of selection, or the survival of the fittest.'

There was only one more book to come and it seemed to have no connection with any of his others. According to Darwin, it was 'a curious little book' on a subject which was his 'hobby horse'. *The Formation of Vegetable Mould, through the Action of Worms, with Observations on their Habits* (October 1881) had nothing to do with evolution, selection or variation; but it still emphasized, like his books on flowers, the interrelationships of organisms: the dependence of animals on plants, plants on animals. The *Worms* grew out of a paper he had read to the Geological Society in 1838 – 'On the Formation of Mould' – in which he described how a scattering of cinders on the ground would end up, a few years later, several inches below the ground. He suggested that worms did it. Years passed before critics denied the likelihood of such an extraordinary hypothesis. Worms, they said, could not possibly turn over that amount of soil; and worms, in large numbers, occurred only in humid soils. Darwin believed that worms could shift large amounts of any soil and he kept pots of soil in his study to confirm it. The worms turned over the soil in the pots and Darwin became more and more fascinated.

Worms had two messages for the reader: worms were 'intelligent' and their activity had amazing results. He showed that worms were sensitive to light, rather like plants, for they had no eyes. They had an instinct to crawl upwards in wet weather and downwards in dry. And they had the ability to plug the burrow with leaves. From an experiment with slips of paper, he discovered that worms generally seized the narrow ends of the slips to plug the burrow. That, he argued, indicated that worms had a certain intelligence.

Apart from some papers on ants and termites – and the ways in which insects fertilized flowers – Darwin had not shown much practical interest in the habits of wild animals. In his major work, he chose most of his analogies from domestic animals. But the little worm became a fascinating animal in Darwin's book and the book was a great success. The book was of interest to the farmer, the archaeologist and the geologist. Without worms, the soil would not be turned and aerated, the leaves not buried and recycled. He calculated that worms made casts at the rate of eight to eighteen tons an acre a year and the whole of the soil's upper layer passed through worms every few years. Before the invention of the plough, it was worms that ploughed the land. Farmers should protect worms. It was worms, too, that buried objects for the archaeologist. Ancient pavements and pots and even buildings were buried. Soft rocks passed through worms: the casts blew away on the wind, got swept away in water. Worms assisted in moulding the profile of the earth, one more factor for Lyell's geology. Darwin's last book, like his first, was geological. Worms, like corals, played an important part in the history of the earth. Darwin's life's work was neatly tied up.

7. On the Bandwagon

'It may be asked how far I extend the doctrine of the modification of species,' Darwin 1859.

In forty-five years Darwin had written nineteen books and some eighty articles and established a lasting reputation for himself and was given the final honour of burial in Westminster Abbey.

Why was Darwinism – the name given to the theory by Wallace – such a success?

Erasmus Darwin, Lamarck, Lyell and Spencer – and the *Vestiges* – had reached the public long before the publication of the *Origin*. Science had already become part of everyday life: steam boats and railways, suspension bridges and tunnels. Scientists had lit the streets with gas, anaesthetized the sick and telegraphed messages across the country. Scientists had increased crop yields and improved livestock. Everyone had to be a scientist 'these days' – even poets: 'if you intend to be a poet', the dean instructed Alton Locke in Kingsley's novel (1850), 'you must become a scientific man. Science has made vast strides and introduced new modes of looking at nature, and poets must live up to the age.'

Science was providing the means of social change as populations shifted from the country to the town. The old distinctions between classes became blurred as newly rich industrialists clambered into the middle classes. Economists preached a land of opportunity. It was a time for individual advancement. The demand for science education increased accordingly. It came from both sexes and all ranks of society.

Change was in the air and evolutionary theory much in the mind. Disraeli's novel *Tancred* had been published in 1847. In 1850, Tennyson published *In Memoriam*. The poet was torn between the joys of religion and the sorrows of evolution. Natural laws and Lyellian geology turned man to fossil and dust.

> Man, her last work, who seem'd so fair . . .
>
> Who trusted God was love indeed
>   And love Creation's final law –
>   Tho' Nature, red in tooth and claw
> With ravine, shriek'd against his creed –
>
> Who loved, who suffer'd countless ills,
>   Who battled for the True, the Just,
>   Be blown about the desert dust,
> Or seal'd within the iron hills?

In 1852, a London undergraduate – the future economist W. S. Jevons – confessed to his diary that, as far as he understood it, he believed in evolution: 'that all animals have been transformed out of one primitive form by the continued influence, for thousands and perhaps millions of years, of climate, geography, etc. Lyell makes great fun of Lamarck's, that is of this theory, but appears to me not to give any good reason against it.' In the *Saturday Review* of 1853, Fitzjames Stephen – Virginia Woolf's uncle – was resigned: 'what difference can it make whether millions of years ago our ancestors were semi-rational baboons.'

Darwin was already known as the author of the popular *Beagle* journal. So well known, in fact, that Alton Locke dreamt he was 'a mylodon among South American forests – a vast sleepy mass, my elephantine limbs and yard-long talons contrasting strangely with the little meek rabbit's head'. They even put Darwin in a novel: Bulwer-Lytton had him with his limpets in *What will he do with it? By Pisistratus Caxton* (1859).

With all the advance publicity before the publication of the book, the *Origin* dropped into history with a bang.

Who read the thousands of copies that were on the market by

January 1860? Who bought a book on evolutionary theory? The book was in demand on the platform at Waterloo Bridge railway station. Darwin's book was read by thousands because it produced in people's minds 'a kind of pleasing excitement' and that was because – according to Sedgwick – 'anything very much opposed to prevailing notions must be a grand *discovery*.' Darwin thought it would appeal because 'the general public appreciates a good dose of reasoning or generalisation, with new and curious remarks on habits, final cause, etc., etc., far more than do the regular naturalists.' But the public reaction was far from rational. *On the Origin of Species by Means of Natural Selection* split the public in half. It split the universities. It divided scientist from scientist, churchman from churchman. It divided politicians and artists and the man in the street. It increased the gap between those seeking to preserve the status quo and those seeking change.

More than ninety leading newspapers and periodicals reviewed the *Origin*. The reviews highlighted the schism. The slight majority of dailies carried favourable reviews, the majority of periodicals were hostile. Huxley seized the review space in *The Times* to bring its readers to Darwin's side – at least, temporarily – but the *Daily News* was against. *Nature, Chambers's Journal, Cornhill* and *Theological Review* were for; *Athenaeum, Lancet, Tablet, Christian Observer* and *Zoologist* against. Ellegard's final analysis of review coverage was 49 per cent actively hostile, 25 per cent enthusiastic or polite, and the rest neutral. In general, the more sophisticated the publication, the less likely to be hostile.

The *Origin* was taken up by fiction writers as a gimmick: a peg to hang stories on or a pretext for attacks on materialism. Crazy machines evolved in Samuel Butler's anti-clerical *Erewhon* (1872) though the concept was hardly Darwinian. Adam and Eve evolved from monkeys in *Zit and Zoe* (1886) by Henry Curwen.

Evolutionary theory was the story line of *The Time Machine* (1895) and *The War of the Worlds* (1898) by H. G. Wells who was, of course, trained as a biologist. Jules Verne took his readers on a Lyellian tour through the geological layers of the earth – in *Journey to the Centre of the Earth* (1864) – where they met living fossils and watched a stupendous fight between the giant fish-reptile *Ichthyosaurus* and the long-necked paddle-reptile *Plesiosaurus*. And the rule of natural law prevailed in *The Water Babies* (1863) by Charles Kingsley, a warm supporter of Darwin: 'I am not going to trouble myself to make things,' Mother Nature told the child, 'I sit here and let them make themselves.'

Political writers, too, jumped on the bandwagon of Darwinian theory, sometimes to justify a prevailing philosophy, sometimes in a genuine attempt to find a new political philosophy.

In 1867, one of Bagehot's essays in the *Fortnightly Review* appeared with the title 'Thoughts on the Application of the Principles of Natural Selection'. He noted that, throughout history, strong nations tended to dominate weak nations. Thus, he concluded, the strongest could be regarded as the best. He went on to ask why one nation should be stronger than another but was unable to find a satisfactory answer. Nor could he find a satisfactory selective force for societies. The most important development in human society – according to Bagehot – was the invention of law imposed by authority, Government and Church. It was difficult to see how Bagehot's model provided variation for change by natural selection. The model expressed pre-*Origin* belief: that selection among wild animals was – as William Buckland believed – merely a trimming device to preserve the status quo. Carnivores functioned as population controllers to maintain numbers and qualities as they were at creation. Bagehot, in fact, rejected the idea of variation: nonconformism, he said, was loathsome to revolutionary and conservative governments alike.

Herbert Spencer who, as a thorough-going evolutionist, had been an immediate convert to the theory of natural selection, applied the new selection theory to society. He argued that each man was responsible for his own and no one else's conduct: the strong would survive, the weak go to the wall – the 'survival of the fittest'. Spencer's philosophy of extreme individualism – based on the materialist laissez-faire economics of Adam Smith and John Stuart Mill – easily assimilated Darwinian theory to justify the entrepreneur who succeeded in society at the expense of his slower or less lucky competitors. He who succeeded was, of course, the 'fittest'.

Darwinism – the Darwin-Wallace theory – judged success only by number of offspring that survived to propagate the next generation. Thus, it was the 'average' that would be successful. Only in a changing environment would 'superior' individuals have the edge and contribute more to posterity than the average.

Spencer's philosophy – social Darwinism – argued that success for the individual was the key to survival, success would be favoured by selection. But there was no reason to suppose that the economically successful individual would leave more offspring than his less successful competitors. If anything, the reverse: Galton found, for example, that heiresses – rich, therefore successful – were comparatively infertile. Social Darwinism had echoes of pre-*Origin* Tennyson.

But, social Darwinism – with all the misleading implications of the title – was enthusiastically imported into the United States of America where it had more influence than in Europe. The American constitution guaranteed the individual's inalienable right to freedom from interference by government. Laissez-faire economics were the order of the day so – in the eyes of America's capitalists – Darwinian theory was the philosophy of capitalism. William Sumner, Professor of Political Economy and Social Science at Yale, formalized the American attitude to Darwinism when he wrote that 'millionaires are a product of natural selection acting on the whole of men to pick out those who can meet the requirement of certain work to be done.' Sumner believed that social competition was a natural law. The great tycoons of American business pictured themselves as successful survivors in the struggle for existence. The transatlantic brand of

Darwinism reached its climax with Spencer's visit to America in 1882. After that, it became modified by the theory of the inheritance of acquired characters which was used to justify improved social conditions. By 1893, Spencer had abandoned Darwinism as a useful guide to social evolution. 'The Doctrine of Evolution', he wrote, 'has not furnished guidance to the extent I had hoped. Most of the conclusions, drawn empirically, are such as right feelings, enlightened by cultivated intelligence, have already sufficed to establish.'

Only in militarist Germany – where natural selection and survival of the fittest swept the country – did social Darwinism persist into the twentieth century. Nazi racial theories owed more to Herder, Nietzsche and Galton than Darwin. But Hitler commanded: 'the stronger must advance and not blend with the weaker, thus sacrificing his own greatness.' In the male struggle for females, the strong would triumph – the weak and sickly would go under in the daily struggle for bread – thus only the strong would survive to propagate the strong. Nietzsche, in fact, condemned Darwinism as a doctrine of mediocrity.

Diametrically opposed political theorists attempted to make the most of evolutionary theory.

George Bernard Shaw presented himself as an anti-Darwinist – but, nevertheless, managed to assimilate some evolutionary theory into his politics. He believed, like all Fabians, in gradualism: evolution not revolution. Shaw argued that, by improving the environment, there would be feedback into the heritable component of the population.

But Darwinian theory – attractive though it was to Fabians – was decidedly at odds with socialist ideology on the subject of individualism. Sidney Webb reconciled Darwinism to socialism in much the same way as Huxley, G. E. Moore and Wallace had done: by supposing that it was not individuals but social groups that evolved, that were selected. He stated categorically: 'the units selected are not individuals but societies.' He did not believe, however, that such selection could account for human society's present condition: 'its action at early stages,' he wrote, 'though analogous, is quite dissimilar.' Beatrice Webb found Darwinism too pessimistic. She could not accept that society had evolved without a preconceived goal. She refused to regard survival as a whim of chance.

But there was one nineteenth-century socialist who managed to reconcile evolutionary theory with his political ideas. Wallace had been influenced in his youth by Robert Owen and passionately believed that social conditions should be improved. He advocated universal education, land nationalisation and a command economy of government-controlled trade. Through such measures society would gradually improve. He did not believe that the good effects would be heritable but, equally, the bad effects would not be heritable either. 'If it is thought that this non-inheritance of the results of education and training is prejudicial to human progress we must remember that on the other hand it also prevents the continuous degradation of humanity by the inheritance of those vicious practices.' Wallace believed, like Huxley, that further human evolution would be cultural rather than physical but – contrary to his earlier unfavourable view of Darwinian sexual selection – he suggested that educated woman's choice of mate would lead to a general improvement in the innate characteristics of the race. Wallace's socialism was interesting because it was totally reconciled with his biological theory. Individual variation, he reasoned, occurred in man as in other animals: therefore, all men were not equal. But granting that biological fact, he advocated that all men should be given an equal opportunity to develop whatever potential they had inherited. Wallace believed that only a combination of good heredity and good environment would produce the best.

There was no doubt that blind evolution by natural selection found its supporters but it found its attackers, too. Anti-religious materialism, blind selection and change without plan were denounced in the novels of Mrs Humphrey Ward. Many of the attacks by popular novelists were at the expense of science as such but natural selection and the reign of higgledy-piggledy was the specific target in Butler's later works. His change of mind – after his early enthusiasm for evolving machines – was largely the result of his personal antagonism to Darwin. He accused Darwin of stealing ideas that had already been fully worked out by Buffon, Erasmus Darwin and Lamarck. Butler picked out Buffon's hints on transmutation but failed to mention that Buffon had recanted.

Literary antipathy towards natural selection – on account of its lack of ultimate aim – lasted into the twentieth century in the writings of George Bernard Shaw. In the famous preface to *Back to Methuselah* (1921), Shaw denounced Darwinism with his usual malice: natural selection, he wrote, was 'a blasphemy, possible to many for whom Nature is nothing but a casual aggregation of inert and dead matter, but eternally impossible to the spirits and souls of the righteous.' Shaw was incensed because Darwin had diminished the power of mind over matter and taken design out of the universe. Chance in evolution – or the 'accident' – indicated the unnaturalness of natural selection. 'Since nothing,' wrote Shaw, 'is more unnatural than an accident. If it could be proved that the whole universe had been produced by such selection, only fools and rascals could bear to live.' But chance was not the main theme in evolutionary theory. Variation was chance – though Darwin did not accept it (that had to wait for Mendel). Selection was adaptive. It had no ultimate aim – there was no ultimate goal – but selection ensured adaptation to circumstances.

Evolution and natural selection were not the only popular targets for fiction and propaganda. Innate variation and the inheritance of acquired characters attracted just as much attention.

The inheritance of acquired characters in the Darwinian sense of a source of variation provided plenty of fun. The doctor in R. D. Blackmore's novel – *The Remarkable History of Tommy Upmore* (1884) – expressed the hope that he would be able to make humans with tails by simply preventing them from ever sitting down. Similar devices gave the elephant's child his trunk, the camel his 'humph', the Ethiopian his black skin and the leopard his spots and that, delightfully, was that. They had done it. There was no prospect of further change, of evolution: 'they will never do it again, Best Beloved, they are quite contented as they are' (Kipling, 1924).

Less humorously, Butler played with inheritance in the autobiographical *The Way of All Flesh* (1903); and, in *Life and Habit* (1910), expressed an extraordinary amalgam of Darwinian and Lamarckian views with a good deal of Bergsonian *élan vital* to carry it along. Hereditary traits were transmitted through inherited organic memory: 'if there had been no such memory, the amoeba of one generation would have exactly resembled the amoeba of the preceding.' Adaptive selection had long since dropped from his philosophy. Shaw, too, was Lamarckist – though, how serious, it was difficult to say. Natural selection had been condemned, Lamarckism was satirized. 'If you have no eyes, and want to see, and keep trying to see, you will finally get eyes . . . solely by willing.' But such an acquisition was not, according to Shaw in *Man and Superman* (1903), passed on to future generations except in infinitesimal amounts. There was no evolution and certainly no selection. Only the Life Force, the *élan vital*, could make changes: new philosophers for old, new brains for dead brains.

In works of fiction, Darwin's theory of acquired characters seemed to support Lamarckism. Inheritance of acquired characters had its political supporters, too. Socialism generally and Marxism particularly took up the idea in a big way, though whether from Darwin or from Lamarck it was difficult to know.

Marx himself, on the one hand preaching revolution, advocated, on the other, a form of evolution: that changing social systems changed political and economic systems and that they, in reverse, changed social systems and so on. This owed more to Hegelian dialectic than Darwinism but Marx thought highly of the *Origin*: 'Darwin's book is very important,' he wrote, 'and it suits me well that it supports the class struggle in history from the point of view of natural science. One has, of course, to put up with the crude English method of discourse.' It was a materialist theory that incorporated the idea of change over a period of time and selected from variations brought about by the environment. But that was about as far as it could go to provide an argument for Marxism, as Engels was the first to see. Dialectical materialism was change and movement over a period of time but it was far from gradualism. Slow adaptation was to be followed by sudden change – revolution – not only to produce a new kind of society but one antithetic to the previous one. No such Hegelian dialectic would be found in Darwinian theory. But Darwinism was not to be dropped from the programme of Marxist teaching in Russia. Gradualism and individual variation would be ignored, change and materialism and inheritance of acquired characters accepted. But Russia's rejection of the Mendelian theory of inheritance – which became part of twentieth-century neo-Darwinism – would lead to the bizarre catastrophe of Lysenkoist agricultural policies.

It was all good publicity.

Darwinism was exciting: it was new, it was fashionable. Everyone read the *Origin* and picked out bits to satirize, bits to use. 'He had the luck to please everybody who had an axe to grind,' snarled Shaw. But in spite of its popularity, Darwinism did not emerge in its totality as any new social or political philosophy. The *Origin* seemed to have the same effect on its political readers as on its author. 'I read years ago', Darwin wrote to Wallace in 1881, 'some books on political economy and they produced a disastrous effect on my mind.'

8. The Soul

'To my mind it accords better with what we know of the laws impressed on matter by the Creator, that the production and extinction of the past and present inhabitants of the world should have been due to secondary causes, like those determining the birth and death of the individual,' Darwin 1859.

The Church of England had a problem in 1859 when the *Origin* became a bestseller. It was a rude shock. The Darwin-Wallace theory was heretical: it denied creation, it postulated a vast time scale, it produced evidence of change, it rejected a Divine Plan in the universe, it presented man as an animal.

The *Origin* shocked the religious mind because Darwin interpreted the world by natural events. He rejected miracles, sought natural causes, found new laws of nature. The static world became dynamic and time took on a new magnitude.

On the nineteenth-century bookshelf the *Origin* was a good companion to works of the German bible critics. In Germany, scholars had interpreted and questioned inconsistencies that arose from treating the Bible as an historical document and the full impact of German criticism struck England in 1835 when George Eliot translated David Strauss's *Leben der Jesu*. In 1860, English scholars – like Baden Powell and Benjamin Jowett – acclaimed the German historical approach in the controversial *Essays and Reviews*.

Essays and Reviews caused almost as much of a stir in England as the *Origin* – and received almost as much attention from the irate Bishop Wilberforce. Baden Powell – who had endorsed the *Origin* as a sound argument for the origination of species by natural causes – did not appeal to Darwinian theory in his essay but rejected miraculous interpretations of events which, he claimed, could be interpreted historically. Jowett, too, called for a rational approach towards the scriptures. Other essays described changes in religious attitudes as historical events.

The dogmatists were outraged: outraged by *Essays and Reviews*, outraged by the *Origin*. The Bible was not history. Man and the universe were not subject to natural laws: certainly not to laws of chance, the 'law' of selection. 'The flood gates of infidelity are open', the dogmatists roared, 'and Atheism overwhelming is upon us.' Nothing so rationally ordered as the universe could be the result of blind selection. Man and the universe, said John Herschel, could not be formed by 'the law of higgledy piggledy'. It was 'the vilest and beastliest paradox ever invented' and 'absolutely incompatible with the work of God'. And the Oxford declaration of 1864, signed by eleven thousand Anglican clergymen, declared that the Bible and its miracles must be taken literally. Creation – not evolution – was the key to the origin of the universe.

Only Unitarians – Darwin's wife Emma Wedgwood was a Unitarian – were immediately open to Darwinism and went so far as to accept not only that evolution might have occurred but also that man might have been part of that evolution.

Gradually the furore in the Protestant Church died down and churchmen came to terms with at least some parts of evolutionary theory. The Bible could be seen as an allegory; a dramatic rendering of facts, both scientific and historical. The Protestant Church – based more on faith than authority – could discriminate between what it would accept and what not accept, literally, from the Bible. It was a personal faith where the individual was answerable only to God. The Protestant Church was hostile to dogmatic interpretations of phenomena. It could not matter less whether man had been created or whether he had evolved from monkeys. In 1896, Frederick Temple, the Headmaster of Rugby – one of the contributors to *Essays and Reviews* and a known supporter of evolution and scientific method – was appointed Archbishop of Canterbury and, thenceforth, as far as the Church of England was concerned, the idea of evolution, including the evolution of man, had to be lived with. Even Gladstone, from an initial repugnance, had come to accept evolution: 'the doctrine of evolution, if it is true, enhances in my judgment the proper idea of the Greatness of God.' The Church of England, however, did not adopt an official attitude to evolution.

Methodists stuck to the doctrine of creation and fundamentalism gained considerable influence in America. In 1925, a law was passed in Tennessee – barring the teaching of evolution in state schools – which led to the famous, or infamous, Scopes trial later that year. John Scopes was a teacher who continued to teach the theory of organic evolution after the law was passed. He did, therefore, break the law and was found guilty. But, despite the verdict, evolutionary teaching continued in other states and, in 1967, the Tennessee law was repealed.

The miracle of creation – the literal interpretation of the Bible – prevented the Catholic Church, too, from accommodating the opinions of the *Origin*. The Catholic Church, in fact, responded only slowly to the evolutionary hypothesis and did not take public issue with Darwin until the appearance of *The Descent of Man*. Individual Catholics – like Mivart – had expressed personal antipathy. But, in the latter part of the century, official decrees were issued discouraging any discussion of evolution. Darwin, however, did not appear on the Index: his books were not prohibited reading like those of his grandfather, Erasmus Darwin. But the proclamation of the infallibility of the Pope in 1870 – and later encyclicals announcing the infallibility of the Bible – discouraged open discussion of Darwinian theory. There was to be no compromise with the new science. It was not until 1951 – when Pope Pius XII relaxed the dogmatic interpretation of the Bible – that open discussion of evolution became officially condoned. In 1951, specific reference was made to evolution in the encyclical but the Catholic 'should not take it for granted', it warned, 'that evolution is a proved fact.'

The biological idea of change and the evolutionary requirement of geological change was inimical to the Church. Both

theories – Darwin's and Lyell's – required an immense time scale
for changes to occur and yet the Bible taught that everything had
been created in seven days. Even if days were interpreted
liberally the Bible did not allow much time for evolution. As long
ago as 1665, Bishop Ussher had proclaimed the Beginning
precisely at 9 a.m., 23 October 4004 BC. It was well outside
Lyell's 'conservative' estimate of at least 240 million years since
the beginning of the earth, and even outside Lord Kelvin's
'ultra-conservative' and probably religiously prejudiced estimate
of 20 million years. The Darwin-Wallace theory was asking for
even more – some 500 million years. This was in no way
acceptable to adherents of a literal interpretation of the Bible.
But there were some who, believing in miracles and supporting
revelation, were, nevertheless, willing to consider the idea of an
ancient earth. Whewell and Sedgwick were opposed to
Darwinian theory, because it rejected a Plan and man's special
status, but were willing to abandon the Flood and extend the age
of the earth. Even willing to allow that – after creation – a self-
evolving system was responsible for at least some of the earth's
animals.

In the latter half of the nineteenth century, many religious
sects in England compromised on evolutionary theory. But man
was still a problem. It was man's place in the universe that had
raised such an uproar in the early days of the *Origin*. It was man's
place in the universe that had attracted so large an audience to the
1860 debate between Huxley and Wilberforce. It was man's place
in the universe that had provoked all the insults even though the
Origin made only two little hints that evolution by natural
selection might apply to man. With the publication of *Man's
Place in Nature* by Huxley and *The Antiquity of Man* by Lyell,
both in 1863 – and *The Descent of Man* in 1871 – man's animal
nature could hardly be denied.

The ancient human remains that were turning up in caves and
quarries had been accepted – even by so staunch a religious
conservative as Lyell – as ancestral to modern man. Such finds

made man's special status more and more difficult to sustain. It became almost impossible when Eugène Dubois discovered, in 1891, a fossil man in Java that was seemingly a missing link between modern man and apes. Impossible for most scientists but not impossible for those who believed in man's soul. Man might have evolved physically from lower animals to a point in time when, say, he walked upright. But the finishing touch to man was his soul. In no way could that be accounted for by natural selection. Even staunch evolutionists like Wallace, Henry Sidgwick and Romanes had trouble with man's soul. Wallace and Sidgwick – having renounced orthodox religion – became spiritualists, searching for consciousness beyond the physical world. Romanes postulated mind permeating all physical nature. Haeckel's atoms, the basis of all natural phenomena, had souls. Beliefs that were hardly different in kind from the 1951 papal encyclical: 'in any discussion of evolution the Catholic must take for granted the spiritual soul of man.'

The Divine Plan, with its ultimate goal, proved more difficult to reconcile with Darwinism. Selection acting on variation without direction was anarchic. It was more the lack of plan – the hazard of selective evolution – that made Darwin's theory unsatisfactory to his contemporaries who were, otherwise, willing to accept it. It was the greatest obstacle for Sedgwick and Whewell because it repudiated all 'reasoning from final causes'. On the whole – explicitly or implicitly – established religion, when it came to terms with evolution, clung to directional evolution towards a goal determined by the Creator at the beginning of the world. It was the Jesuit palaeontologist Pierre Teilhard de Chardin who attempted the reconciliation of Darwinian theory with a Plan.

The Phenomenon of Man was published in 1959, four years after Teilhard de Chardin's death. It claimed to be strictly scientific. Teilhard de Chardin accepted the evolutionary process – accepted it as an explanation of the universe, the earth and all life including man. But he introduced into the universe a consciousness – present in the molecular constituents of the universe – that, like matter, could evolve. With the origin of human consciousness, consciousness entered the era of the 'noosphere'. The consciousness of the noosphere would continue to evolve until it became the 'christosphere'. This ultimate consciousness, having lost all connection with matter, would occupy no space and could be represented as a point: the famous 'omega point' of Teilhard de Chardin's philosophy. The point was Christ.

Time, man's animal nature, aimless evolution – all presented problems and few of Darwin's contemporaries were willing to accept them all and break with religion. Darwin argued that man had evolved by means of natural selection and sexual selection and that special attributes, like speech, had been part of that evolution. He rejected the idea of an evolutionary goal: 'if I saw an angel coming down to teach us good, and I was convinced from others seeing him that I was not mad, I should believe in design' – but he did not rule out an initial creation. Darwin abandoned religion but brought up his children in the Church of England. Like Huxley, Galton, Tylor and Lubbock, he believed that life was bearable without religion. Like them, Darwin preferred scientific interpretations of natural phenomena. He believed in the evolutionary explanation of man's 'spiritual' component and argued, like J. S. Mill, that religious experience was hallucination.

Scientific naturalism, as it was called, survived into the twentieth century when it appeared as scientific humanism and found an advocate in T. H. Huxley's grandson. Julian Huxley – in *New Bottles for New Wine* (1957) – declared that man's evolution was not predestined but controlled by man himself. Thus, it could be directed towards man's self-realization. The ethical goal was happiness and freedom. 'Man's most sacred duty,' he wrote, 'and at the same time his most glorious opportunity, is to promote the maximum fulfilment of the evolutionary process on this earth.'

9. Missing Links

'He who believes that each being has been created as we now see it, must occasionally have felt surprise when he has met with an animal having habits and structure not at all in agreement,' Darwin 1859.

Darwin considered himself a man of science. He regarded the repercussions of the *Origin*, outside the scientific world, as extraordinary. But biologists were as much divided – on what was, after all, a biological theory – as the general public.

Hooker and Huxley, forewarned, were immediate converts to the Darwin-Wallace theory of evolution by natural selection, supported by a massive array of facts in the *Origin*. James Lubbock (Lord Avebury), Henry Bates, Asa Gray, Robert Chambers – author of the *Vestiges* – and Herbert Spencer soon joined them. Lyell – on whose geological theories the *Origin* depended – was doubtful. He was not against but, equally, not for it. He was not convinced that natural forces – similar to those that changed the face of the earth – could account for biological changes. Against the *Origin*, as Darwin told Hooker in March 1860, was: 'one large class of men, more especially I suspect of naturalists, never will care about *any* general question, of which old Gray, of the British Museum, may be taken as a type; and secondly, nearly all men past a modest age, either in actual years or in mind, are, I am fully convinced, incapable of looking at facts under a new point of view.' Darwin saw that it would be an 'uphill fight'.

'Dear old' Adam Sedgwick wrote Darwin an indignant letter and reviewed him 'savagely and unfairly' in the *Spectator*. Louis Agassiz – the Swiss palaeontologist – considered the transmutation theory 'a scientific mistake'. Richard Owen did not declare himself but provided others with ammunition against it.

Darwinism, skilfully advertised by Haeckel, persuaded the

German biologists – but not von Baer. In France, *le darwinisme* was never to become respectable.

Eventually, however, the theory of evolution by natural selection unified biology and became a working hypothesis for further work. In April 1880, Huxley was able to say in 'The Coming of Age of the Origin of Species' – a lecture in London to the Royal Institution – that 'evolution is no longer a speculation, but a statement of fact'.

But palaeontologists continued to have problems and the biggest problem was the 'imperfection of the geological record'. Were missing links missing because they were not found or were they genuine gaps between groups of animals? Missing links had been useful evidence for catastrophism. For Cuvier, there had been several creations, each one destroyed by a catastrophe: fire, earthquake or flood. There was no connection between each creation except the hand of the Creator. 'Whole races were destroyed forever, leaving only a few relics which the naturalists can scarcely recognize.' There were mastodons in one creation, flooded to extinction. Elephants replaced them in the next creation. There was no lineal connection between the two.

Darwin was well aware that without a record of gradual transformation running through the rocks the palaeontological record was not good evidence of evolution. But, he argued, the absence of a neat series could be accounted for in several ways. There might be, for example, no intermediate between two animals because each had been derived independently from a common ancestor. There might be no apparent intermediate because a change might have occurred in many morphological features at the same time, on the hypothesis of correlation of parts. There might be no intermediate because a group had migrated in from somewhere else. But Darwin believed that, in the final analysis, missing links were the result of the imperfection of the fossil record and he was confident that intermediates would eventually be found to fill the gaps. Missing ancestral mammals had turned up in the jurassic (150 million years ago) – in the Stonesfield slate near Oxford, in the 1820s.

On gaps, Huxley was not convinced. However closely man might resemble gorilla there was, for example, a considerable gap between them: a gap similar to the gaps in the fossil record. Gaps prevented Huxley from wholeheartedly accepting gradual evolution.

Perhaps there were occasions, he worried, when there had been sudden jumps just as the *Vestiges* claimed. 'You have loaded yourself with an unnecessary difficulty,' he wrote to Darwin in November 1859, 'in adopting *Natura non facit saltum* so unreservedly.' Huxley puzzled how modern one-toed horses *Equus* could have evolved from a three-toed fossil known as *Anchitherium* 'near animal' from miocene days (25 million years ago) and how that animal, in its turn, could have evolved from *Hyracotherium* 'coney animal' described by Owen. There were gaps. But, in Huxley's example, the situation was clarified in just the way Darwin had predicted. Finds in North America – by O. C. Marsh – started to fill the gaps in the 1870s and, as more and more fossils turned up, an evolutionary trend could be discerned: from small horses with four toes and low-crowned teeth to horses with three toes and high-crowned teeth; to horses with only the middle of the three toes touching the ground and high-ridged constantly growing teeth; and, finally, to the big modern horse with only one toe and even bigger teeth. Little three-toed horses evolved in a straight line to big one-toed horses. There – in horses – was the gradualism that Darwin and Huxley were looking for: a straight line of evolutionary development.

In no time, there were straight lines being found in all sorts of fossil lineages. Orthogenesis, or straight-line evolution, became an important part of evolutionary theory. There were the extinct horse-related titanotheres 'giant animals' which, from small eocene beginnings (50 million years ago) in North America, grew bigger and bigger and developed blunt horns on their noses. There were no horns on the early small animals: then, there were small nasal knobs; then, by the early oligocene (35 million years ago) the knobs had become horns and reached their biggest and most complex form in the elephant-sized *Brontotherium* 'thunder animal'. That was the end of the line. The Irish elk followed a similar pattern in Europe: getting bigger and bigger from the pliocene (7 million years ago) to the pleistocene (1 million years ago) with bigger and bigger antlers until it could no longer hold its head up and dropped down dead – so the story went. Those spectacular trends were not confined to mammals. There were several lines of oysters that developed coiling in one shell. The coiling increased steadily until the coiled shell pressed so firmly on the other shell that the oyster could no longer open and the line became extinct.

Orthogenesis – leading in a straight line to extinction – could not be adaptive. It was, many argued, an indication of an innate force – an example of evolution unassociated with natural selection – the 'life force' that the French philosopher, Henri Bergson, had described in *L'Evolution Créatrice* in 1907. The *élan vital* was the cause of all evolution. But more and more fossils appeared and – through a reinterpretation of new finds – the straight line was modified into a branching tree.

During the 1940s, G. G. Simpson was able to show a branching tree, instead of a straight line, in horse evolution. The original North American small horse gave rise to many new forms by divergence. They spread all over the world, some of them bigger and some of them smaller. *Hyracotherium* evolved into horses with three toes and high-crowned teeth. But, again, some were bigger and some were smaller. And so it went on to even bigger horses: horses with only one toe and with high-crowned, heavy-ridged teeth. But not all were evolving in exactly the same way at exactly the same time. There was an orthogenetic trend but that overall trend, Simpson showed, was an average of many trends and a superficial interpretation of the facts. There was no indication of an inner urge – or *élan vital* – but a pattern of adaptation by natural selection. The first horses, he estimated, lived in the forest: eating fruits and flabby leaves, rather like the

Malaysian mouse-deer. Conditions changed – the forest decreased or, within the forest, competition increased – and the horses took to living in open woodland, browsing on hard leaves. Selection favoured bigger size for reaching branches and better teeth for chewing hard leaves. Then grass brought the horses out into the open – on to the plains – exposed to carnivores. It became advantageous to run fast. Long legs were better than short legs but long legs were heavy: less heavy, however, with only one toe. Grass was tough and big rough teeth would be favoured.

Simpson rejected *élan vital* and rejected orthogenesis as a description of horse evolution. Divergent speciation by natural selection accounted for horse evolution.

But the rocks record many animals trending to large size – titanotheres, Irish elk, sabre-tooth tigers – and many of them became extinct. Could all trends be explained on Simpson's model: selection to fit new circumstances?

There is some justification for supposing that large size can be an adaptation to physiological independence of the environment. The bigger the animal, the less the heat loss and the less energy consumed, for example. The bigger the animal, the more cells it has. Large size goes with long life and a small number of offspring. Large size is a good thing provided that there is plenty of food about and plenty of room. But what if the environment changes? The food source may be restricted: the large animal has nothing to eat and nowhere to go. Worse, slow turnover of offspring will not provide varieties quickly enough for selection to adapt the population to the changed conditions.

Change in climate, change in food supply might have found the titanotheres, Irish elk and sabre-tooths in just such a situation. There can be inertia in bigness. Sometimes it is better to be small.

Orthogenesis – revamped as Darwinian gradualism – is brought about by natural selection, without any unstoppable innate force directing a lineage to its eventual downfall.

Orthogenesis may have a Darwinian explanation but fossil lineages do not always show gradual change: some seem to stay exactly the same for millions of years. Some European beetles have shown no change during the last million years. The lampshell – living in warm mud – has not changed for five hundred million years. The lampshell may have survived because its muddy environment has always been available in some part of its range. Beetles may have survived because if the climate changed in one place they moved to another, always moving to stay in the same sort of conditions. Given a stable selective force, same environment: no change would be expected in lampshell or beetle, according to strict Darwinian theory.

Other oddities of the fossil record can be resolved without resort to anything more spectacular than evolution by natural selection. Gaps, as Darwin predicted, have been filled. But not all gaps: some links are still 'missing'. And some curious situations have occurred. A species has remained constant for thousands of years, changed suddenly to another form – and again remained constant for thousands of years. In 1857, H. Bronn had suggested that that was a common pattern.

Antarctic radiolaria (tiny shelled protozoa) have increased in size suddenly on three separate occasions over a period of two and a half million years. In between the jumps in size there was virtually no change. The sudden changes, it has been argued, were due to innate tendencies to size increase and were not necessarily adaptive. On this showing, a new species – or even a new genus – could come into existence suddenly and then either become extinct or stay unchanged until the next sudden event. This, the authors said, proves Darwin was wrong: no slow accumulation of small variations, no gradual adaptation to the conditions of existence, no slow evolution by natural selection.

New fossils related to modern man have fuelled the controversy. *Homo erectus* was found in Java in 1891 and Pekin man – who turned out to belong to the same species as Java man – was found in the 1930s. In 1925, the first *Australopithecus* 'southern ape' was found in South Africa. The skull shape of *Australopithecus* – and the position of the big hole through which the spinal cord passed from the brain – was more like man's than ape's. The hole lay under the base of the skull, indicating that *Australopithecus* walked upright: a deduction later confirmed by the discovery of a pelvis, ankle joints and foot bones. And *Australopithecus* was more like man than ape in tooth and lower jaw shape. More and more *Australopithecus* were found and at least two species were distinguished: *A. robustus* was a heavy-jawed chap, adapted to chewing up vegetation; and *A. africanus* was more lightly built, an omnivore. Four species of the genus *Homo* were found. *H. habilis* may have been the first man to use tools. *H. erectus* – found later in Africa as well as in Asia – had a thick skull and big teeth. *H. neanderthalensis* had a big flattish skull and was a cold weather man. *H. sapiens* – about 100,000 years old – is the current species. All the fossils related to modern man lay within the last five million years of geological time: before that, there is a gap.

The hominid lineage has been interpreted as an example of evolution by saltation, by jumps. It seems from the record that the earliest *Australopithecus* species and *Homo habilis* were contemporary. Thus, the argument goes, they had leapt suddenly – fully differentiated, without intermediates – from unknown ancestors. Once arrived, the argument continues, they did not change until *Homo habilis* leapt into *H. erectus* who, in turn, leapt into *H. neanderthalensis* and *H. sapiens*, simultaneously. The hominid lineage was a demonstration of evolution by saltation, punctuated equilibrium. *Natura facit saltum*, as Huxley would have said and Darwin would have denied.

There may, however, be other explanations of the same material. New dating makes *Homo habilis* more recent than the earliest *Australopithecus*. Early *Australopithecus*, therefore, could have evolved into *Homo habilis* by gradual evolution. By gradualism, *H. habilis* could have become *H. erectus* and, then, *H. neanderthalensis* and *H. sapiens*. The slow increase in brain size and the slow increase in weight – from the 28 kg of *Australopithecus* to the 58 kg of modern man – are evidence of gradualism. With new dating, man can still have evolved in a typically Darwinian fashion.

But supposing species really do come into existence suddenly, in one jump? Is there any biological explanation? What sort of leaping theory could account for them?

From recent mathematical analysis of the shell forms of tiny fossil protozoa a stepped evolutionary sequence has been obtained. There is continuity but no sign of gradual change, only abrupt changes. The pattern could be attributed not to some inner force or act of creation but to rapid changes in the oceanic tides. If environment changes rapidly, then it is not surprising that species change rapidly – or become extinct.

A model for sudden change by selection has been based on catastrophe theory (not Cuvierian catastrophe). It is supposed that an animal is adapted to some environmental factor – such as mean annual temperature – which varies steadily in one direction, south to north of a stretch of land. The animal starts in the south and expands north. Small size is selected at the southern end of the range. Individuals in the population range from small to medium, in a normal one-humped distribution curve. As the animal spreads north – to cooler surroundings – large size becomes equally advantageous: small size is still advantageous for hiding, say; but large size is advantageous for thermal efficiency. Medium size is of no advantage. The size distribution curve is two-humped. Further spread into the cool north takes the species into a place where thermal efficiency becomes more advantageous than hiding. Thus, there is a sudden unidirectional selection for large size: the population flips over to a new mean value for size. Again, the fossil record would be unlikely to show those changes. The intermediate stages, being less well adapted than either of the extremes, would have had smaller populations and lasted comparatively short periods of time.

Darwin was well aware of this possibility. Changes, he thought, would have been local and, therefore, concerned small populations which would not have expanded until conditions had become suitable. Then, they would have expanded rapidly. It was unlikely, he thought, that small local changes would show up in the fossil record.

But punctuated equilibrium and missing links have been seized on by a new generation of creationists to 'prove' that evolution is not a satisfactory explanation of palaeontological facts.

At the beginning of 1981, the Creation-Science Research Center of San Diego brought a suit against the California State Board of Education to prohibit the teaching of evolution in schools unless the creationist doctrine was also taught. Religion was not taught in American schools but science was. The Creation-Science Research Center either had to prove that creationism was a scientific theory or that evolution was a religion. In 1972, the Creation-Science Research Center had proclaimed its Statement of Belief. It believed that the Bible was the word of a Master Designer and historically and scientifically true. It believed that all living things including man were created according to the description in Genesis and that any evolution that had occurred was a mere modification of the original creations. It believed that the Flood had occurred. The Creationists denied both Lyellian geology and Darwinian biology. They maintained that the details of the Flood should be examined and taught in as much detail as, for example, continental drift. They denied that radioactive decay was an accurate means of dating rocks and fossils. The apparent great age of the earth, they claimed, was the Master Designer's practical joke. They denied that missing links had been found. They asserted that if the second law of thermodynamics were true, then evolution was not possible. The second law of thermodynamics states that entropy is always increasing or, in plain language, everything is always tending towards disorder.

Thus, order and organization can only be built up and maintained by forces which act against this tendency. Natural selection cannot do that. The Master Designer can.

The twentieth-century creationists have tried to give creation a new look by attempting to make it a testable scientific theory. In 1973, the Creation-Science Research Center mounted an expedition to Mount Ararat to look for remains of the Ark. They claimed to have found fossil human footprints alongside dinosaurs. However, the Creation-Science Research Center lost its case because it was unable to convince the court that creation was a scientific theory.

But the repercussions spread far. They have spread to the British Museum of Natural History and permeated recent exhibitions. Not creationist in intent, the display of dinosaurs is arranged according to the fashionable theory of classification by cladistics.

Modern classification follows one of three models. There is evolutionary classification based on lineages. Ancestors and descendants are identified by shared 'primitive' characters, in the temporal sense. Primitive characters are given greater weight in the classification than so-called specialized characters. There is phenetic or numerical classification – advocated in 1763 by Michel Adanson – where organisms are grouped according to characters they have in common regardless of presumed ancestry, without weighting. There is cladistic classification. Relationships are constructed from the number of specialized characters – or derived characters – that groups have in common.

In cladistic classification, branching diagrams are constructed to show relationships between groups. Groups – irrespective of age – are at the tips of the branches. No attempt is made to determine ancestors or to establish a time scale. In a cladogram there can be no ancestors. The objective is to group like with like, not to construct phylogenetic trees.

Cladistics is used by the British Museum of Natural History for its new exhibits. Cladistic layout gives an immediate impression of saltation: new terminal taxa without ancestors. It is great for ideologists and fanatics: for creationists, for Marxists. Out with gradualism, in with saltation: out with evolution, in with revolution. Out with hierarchies and ancestral inheritance, in with equality and no innate variation.

Cladistics – although it has been used as an anti-evolution weapon – is not an evolutionary theory. Cladistics is a method of classification which, ironically, would have appealed to Darwin who advocated classification according to inherited similarities. And Darwin used such classification as evidence of evolution: 'propinquity of descent – the only known cause of the similarity of organic beings – is the bond, hidden as it is by various degrees of modification, which is partially revealed to us by our classification.'

Cladistics – as a method of classification – accords with Darwinian theory: there is no justification for using it as a weapon to undermine Darwinian theory.

Missing links and saltations can be interpreted conventionally: by Darwinian small-variation selection. Some, however, can be large-scale changes in the heritable material – changes misunderstood in Darwin's day. But can large-scale changes in the heritable material direct evolution or is selection the final arbiter?

10. Use and Disuse

'In both varieties and species, use and disuse seem to have produced some effect,' Darwin 1859.

As Weismann's theory of the independence of the germ plasm gained acceptance and the inheritance of acquired characters lost credibility, biologists were forced to look for the causes of variation in the germ cells. The location of variation was narrowed down: first, to the single germ cell contributed by each parent at fertilization; then, to the single nucleus; then, by the 1880s, to the chromosomes within the nucleus. Somewhere in those chromosomes lay the key to heredity.

The initial steps had been taken by Gregor Mendel, in 1866. Like Darwin, he had a copy of Gärtner's book: *Experiments and Observations in Hybridisation in the Plant Kingdom* (1845). Like Darwin, he was aware that domestic plants varied and that new varieties had been selected by man. Mendel had read the German translation of the *Origin* and saw the relevance of his plant hybridization experiments to 'the history of the evolution of organic forms'. In the introduction to his paper – 'Experiments on Plant Hybridisation' (1866) – he remarked that evolution was 'a question the importance of which cannot be overestimated.' But Mendel, unlike Darwin, was well trained in mathematics and German cytology. He knew that only one cell from each parent was involved at fertilization and he was able to assess the consequences in simple mathematical terms. He solved the immediate problem of inheritance and variation.

Mendel demonstrated that correct interpretation of hybridization required that parental contributions should be equal and that blending should not occur. Inherited characters, he argued, were paired and only one of a pair was contributed by a parent to the offspring. Different combinations had different effects: two purple factors produced purple flowers; two white factors, white flowers; and one purple factor and one white factor, purple flowers. The flower's appearance, therefore, did not necessarily express its inherited factors. And what if the purple hybrids were self-fertilized? White flowers – as well as purple flowers – appeared in the progeny. The white factor did not get lost – it was present if not always apparent – and it was not contaminated by blending with the purple factor. Take many factors, he said: each factor would be inherited, independent of all the others. The mathematical combination of indestructible factors in the germ cells was the source of variation.

Blending inheritance, unequal parental contribution, environmentally influenced gemmules had gone. No one took much notice: Mendel's *Experiments* was published before Darwin's *Variation*. Mendel worked with peas and his results were not seen as having application to other plants. The trouble was that Mendel's contemporaries worked with complex cultivated plants – or, like Karl Nägeli, with hawkweeds that appear to be fertilized by incoming pollen but, in fact, do not get fertilized – and the cultivated plants produced a welter of unanalysable variation and hawkweeds none at all. The results did not confirm Mendel's pea experiments. Mendel was disappointed but convinced that his results had general application: '*Mein Zeit will kommen.*' It came with Hugo de Vries in 1900.

There is no evidence that Darwin read Mendel's paper – there were only two copies in England – and, even if he had, it is doubtful whether he would have appreciated its significance. His own experiments had produced similar results: normal and peloric snapdragons, hairy and smooth plants, grey and white mice. He had noted them in *Variation* but consigned them to the list of exceptions to the rule of blending inheritance. Galton had told Darwin that parents contributed equally to the offspring. He demonstrated that pangenesis did not work. He cast doubt on blending inheritance. But Darwin was to believe in unequal parental contribution, blending inheritance and inheritance of acquired characters for the rest of his life.

Just before Darwin's death, in 1882, there was a reference to Mendel in England. George Romanes included Mendel's name in his article 'Hybridism' in the *Encyclopaedia Britannica*. Romanes did not appreciate its significance.

It was not until the Dutchman Hugo de Vries had repeated many of Mendel's experiments – and arrived at the same conclusions – that Mendel's work was 'discovered' or, more accurately, recognized for its true worth. De Vries wrote a book called *Intracellular Pangenesis* in 1889. In it, he stated his belief in pangenesis: pangenes could be mixed together in any proportion and could explain the results of hybridization. The seemingly endless variations in the progeny of hybrids could be accounted for by the mixing of pangenes in various combinations. De Vries continued his experiments. He crossed campions and found that colour behaved in the same way as in Mendel's peas. He crossed poppies and found some characters were masked or recessive to others, as in Mendel's peas. By 1899, de Vries had convinced himself of the particulate nature of heritable factors, of paired factors – and of their segregation and recombination at sexual reproduction – of dominance and of the unchanged continuity of the heritable particles. He had experimented himself out of pangenesis and – like Darwin in 1859 – he had assembled a mass of evidence. He was ready to publish a new theory of the inheritance of variation when a friend sent him – like Wallace to Darwin in 1858 – a copy of Mendel's paper. One version of his new theory had already gone to Paris for publication but he hastily added a note to the German version to the effect that Mendel's work on peas had the same general application as his own work. Two other men came across Mendel's paper at about that time: Carl Correns checking through the literature for evidence of the particulate nature of inheritance – which he had by then discovered – and Erich von Tschermak working on inheritance in peas for his doctorate.

Mendel's laws and de Vriesian confirmation were, for the scientific community, almost as great an event as the *Origin*. William Bateson received a reprint of de Vries's paper, hunted out Mendel's original paper and, in a lecture to the Royal Horticultural Society in London, publicized it immediately.

By this time, of course, everyone knew about chromosomes. There was only one more move to make: to associate Mendelian factors with chromosomes. It was Walter Sutton, in the USA, who achieved this synthesis. Chromosomes were paired, only one of a pair went into each germ cell: therefore, Mendelian factors might be equated with chromosomes. Chromosomes retained their identity – like Mendelian factors – from cell division to cell division. But it was to be years before biologists convinced themselves that Mendelian factors – the genes – kept their identity unaffected by their partners. Blending inheritance was slow to die.

One snag in the Mendelian and de Vriesian theories was that the number of chromosomes could not be exactly equated with the number of factors. Thus, there must be many factors on each chromosome.

The mechanism of inheritance had been solved. But what about variation? Mixing of independent factors could produce variation – up to a point – but it could not go on indefinitely. Variation, declared de Vries, was caused by mutation. A gene could change – in one jump – from one condition to another. Gene mutation and gene recombination was the cause of variation. Mutation was random and spontaneous: it caused such changes in the heritable material that, in one jump, species changed into other species. De Vries had obtained his evidence for large saltatory mutations from work on the evening primrose *Oenothera Lamarckiana*. When a mutation occurred in Lamarck's evening primrose, the offspring, that inherited it, bore a striking resemblance either to the gaudy evening primrose or the downy evening primrose.

Dramatic saltatory de Vriesian mutations went out of fashion shortly after being discovered as biologists turned their attention to the Mendelian factors, or genes.

Genes were found to mutate but the difference between a gene and its mutant form was slight. Normal genes that were responsible for the red pigment in the fruitfly eye mutated to genes which made pink pigment or none at all. Genes determining the colour of pea seeds could mutate from yellow-forming to green-forming. The mutant gene affected the same character as the normal gene; mutations were variations on a theme. Thousands of genes were discovered by studying mutations: genes in plants, genes in flies and, subsequently, genes in man and genes in bacteria and viruses. Genes were carried on the chromosomes: they retained their identity and assembled in new combinations at sexual reproduction.

In the 1920s, mutations were induced artificially by the use of ionizing radiation and, later, by chemicals such as mustard oils. No new mutations were made: inducing agents simply speeded up the process. It confirmed that mutation was random, whether spontaneous or induced. Some genes mutated more often than others but the outcome of an experiment could only be predicted statistically. Some genes had a higher probability of mutating than others. Mutations seemed to be chance, undirected, small-scale events: the raw material of evolution.

What were those genes, strung like beads on a chromosome? It was not until the 1940s that the chemistry of the genes began to be unravelled. Genes were identified as lengths of a comparatively simple molecule which was an integral part of the chromosome, the deoxyribonucleic acid, or DNA. The DNA proved to be a code that carried genetic information from cell to cell and from generation to generation. The code determined the manufacture of proteins like enzymes and the α and β poly-peptide chains that make the blood pigment haemoglobin. A small change in the chemistry of the DNA led to the manufacture of a slightly different protein. A change in the molecule of the gene that specified the β haemoglobin chain led to a change in the chemistry of that chain. The spectacular result was a different haemoglobin called sickle-cell haemoglobin. Although sickle-cell haemoglobin differed only slightly, it caused the red blood cells – normally round – to become sickle-shaped and the haemoglobin was less effective at carrying oxygen. With two sickle-cell genes (homozygous) a carrier died of anaemia, with one sickle-cell gene and one normal gene (heterozygous) there was no problem. The mutation from normal to sickle-cell occurred spontaneously, from time to time: about once in a hundred thousand germ cells. Mutations seemed to occur – at cell division – when the DNA misreplicated. Misreplication seemed to happen by chance.

The simple chemical changes of the genes – the genes caused protein differences between individuals – were the source of small variations for Darwinian evolution.

Subsequently, advances in biochemical techniques detected mutations that had no apparent effect on the individual. Chemical changes in 'unimportant' parts of an enzyme made no difference to that enzyme's activity. Selection would not detect such mutations – they could accumulate. Such mutations were 'neutral'. In theory, neutral genes could exist but, in practice, it is difficult to establish genetic neutrality. Many genes originally thought to be neutral were found to exert an effect which, in fact, could be detected by selection. Changes in 'unimportant' parts of the insulin gene, for example, might be neutral: guinea pigs have a mutant insulin. Was it neutral? The apparently neutral chemical change in the guinea pig gene was found to have widespread consequences. Guinea pig insulin was less effective in sugar-storing powers than, say, bovine insulin but it packed up better – it could be stored in a small space – and it turned out to have a powerful effect in promoting growth.

To prove that an apparently neutral gene had, in fact, distinct effects was one thing. To prove that it had none – was genuinely neutral – was almost impossible. If neutral genes do exist, they provide yet another source of variation: lying around having no effect but available if conditions change to their advantage.

Progress in the understanding of small-scale gene mutations did not lead to total neglect of de Vriesian mutation. De Vriesian mutations in Lamarck's evening primrose had turned out to be due to complex alterations in sets of chromosomes. Lamarck's evening primrose was a garden hybrid – between the gaudy and the downy evening primrose – and, from time to time, the parental sets of chromosomes separated and the original species appeared. In 1929, a curious shoot appeared on a hybrid *Primula* growing in Kew Gardens. The hybrid was sterile but the new shoot had fertile flowers. The new shoot had bigger and more ornamental flowers than the hybrid or the hybrid's parents. The cells of the new shoot were big and had twice as many chromosomes as the hybrid. *Primula kewensis* was a polyploid and a new species. Polyploidy – or the increase in whole sets of chromosomes – was found to be widespread among plants. Polyploid plants with more chromosomes had big cells and were, consequently, big plants. Not surprisingly, many crop plants turned out to be polyploids.

Wheats are polyploid: some, like macaroni wheat, have four sets of original wild wheat chromosomes; the bread wheats have six sets. Apples, cherries, chrysanthemums and tobacco plants are polyploids. Giant polyploid 'tetra' snapdragons have been produced and marketed commercially. Polyploidy is not a peculiarity of cultivated plants: about 70 per cent of grasses are polyploid. In Sweden, 54 per cent of all native flowering plants are polyploid.

Polyploidy is rare in animals. Animals are more affected by cell size than plants because body size is strictly controlled. The monitoring system of a developing animal normally ensures an average-sized adult. Polyploid animals – with fewer cells because polyploid cells are bigger than normal – could be disastrously affected by fewer nerve cells or digestive cells. But some frogs, some worms and a few brine shrimps – living in exceptional circumstances – seem to be polyploids.

Not only polyploidy but anomalies in chromosome number have been found to occur in wild populations of plants and animals. They, too, are a cause of variation.

Some hawksbeards have extra chromosomes which – in contrast to the effects of an extra chromosome in humans of which the commonest example is Down's syndrome or mongolism – do not seem to be, in any way, deleterious to the plant. The majority of house mice have forty chromosomes but there are Swiss populations with numbers from thirty-eight to twenty-two. The reduction has not been brought about by a loss of chromosomes but by end-to-end joining of two chromosomes into one. Similar fusions have occurred in the horse family: the Przewalski wild horse – that once roamed the steppes of Mongolia – has sixty-six chromosomes; the mountain zebra of South Africa, thirty-two. In between, there are domestic horses with sixty-four chromosomes, wild Somali asses with sixty-two, Afghanistan onagers with fifty-six, narrow-striped zebras with forty-six and broad-striped plains zebras with forty-four.

Variations, then, can result from many causes: from the combinations of genes and chromosomes, from gene mutations and chromosome mutations. Variation is random and, to be inherited, it must occur in the germ cells. Only the germ cells are concerned with the next generation. There is no known mechanism by which mutations in body cells can be transmitted to the germ cells.

The inheritance of acquired characters has been replaced by Weismannism and Mendelism and the modern developments. Or has it? The inheritance of acquired characters proves to be a popular and persistent theory of the cause of variation.

Some people continued to believe that if dogs' tails were docked in each generation short tails would eventually be genetically inherited – but the evidence was against them. Such direct and injurious environmental effects were not satisfactory examples of the inheritance of acquired characters. Lamarck had imagined changes being brought about by an animal striving to achieve a new form. The snake became long and narrow 'as a result of repeated efforts at elongation'. Darwin, too, had thought of habits becoming incorporated into the heritable material: 'but when any habit or other mental attribute, or insanity is inherited, we must believe that some actual modification is transmitted,' he wrote, 'and this implies according to our hypothesis that gemmules derived from modified nerve-cells are transmitted to the offspring.'

The inheritance of acquired characters is an attractive theory to anyone interested in behaviour. In the 1920s, learning experiments tested the inheritance of acquired characters in rats. Rats were trained to make a choice between light and dark. The learning, it was claimed, passed to the offspring of the trained rats. The later generations learned the trick more and more quickly. But when the experiments were repeated some years later they did not confirm the original findings. More learning experiments followed. Flatworms were trained to a simple behavioural pattern and their brain-cell nucleic acid injected into untrained flatworms. The nucleic acid of the trained flatworms, it was claimed, conferred the training on the untrained flatworms. Those results, too, were not reproducible.

A laboratory population of fruitflies was subjected to high temperature at a critical moment in the life cycle. The temperature shock caused abnormalities in the wing patterns of about half the population. Individuals with the abnormality were mated and their offspring subjected to the temperature shock. After eighteen generations, the number of individuals with abnormal wing pattern had risen to 90 per cent and, when the temperature treatment was discontinued, the high proportion was maintained. Had an acquired character been inherited? Or had an induced mutation occurred? Curiously, selection had occurred. Genetic investigation ruled out induced mutation as an explanation. Selection had occurred for those flies that were genetically equipped to produce the abnormality in response to the environmental stimulus. Continued selection ensured that the response was increasingly certain until genes for producing the abnormality, without any encouragement from the environment, had been selected into the population. Not inheritance of acquired characters – not induced mutation – but a good demonstration of how sudden adaptive change occurred.

Adaptive change in relative growth rates is another example of selection mimicking Lamarckism. Absence of certain salts in the water might slow the formation of frogs' legs. Some frogs – but not all – might become sexually mature without legs, adult tadpoles. Selection – the water composition – would favour only those tadpoles that were genetically competent to become sexually mature. 'Adult tadpoles' would be a new species. Selection, again: selection for rapid adaptation, selection for saltation.

Inheritance of acquired characters had been explained away again? Not at all. The fruitfly experiment was seized on by the psychologist Jean Piaget as evidence of the incorporation into the gene complex of an adaptively acquired character, in spite of the selective interpretation given by its author.

Abnormal modes of behaviour – formed in response to stress – could, Piaget claimed, be incorporated into the genes. (Inheritance of acquired characters has always appealed to psychologists. Freud was committed to the theory: racial memories were, for him, an important part of human inheritance.) Despite sophisticated reasoning from developmental genetics, however, Piaget did not make it clear how environmental effects got from the site of modification to the germ cells.

But students of behaviour are not the only ones to cling to inheritance of acquired characters. Recently, it has been claimed that immunological tolerance acquired by a male mouse has been passed to the offspring. A tumour virus, or retrovirus, picked up DNA coding for the immunological tolerance from cells that had acquired the tolerance. The virus then took the bits of 'tolerant' DNA to the germ cells, incorporated them – as a retrovirus can do – into the chromosomes and, thus, tolerance was passed on to the offspring. Modern pangenesis, indeed!

Two attempts to repeat the experiments failed and other tests, designed to discover whether acquired immunological tolerance can be inherited, have been equally negative.

Modern genetics has revealed much greater plasticity in the heritable material than anyone suspected. Viruses can insert bits of DNA into cells, some genes can jump from one chromosome to another, bacteria can make enzymes when 'needed'. In the course of evolution, new genes have been made: often, it seems, by stringing together bits and pieces of other genes. None of it supports pangenesis or inheritance of acquired characters, nor does it negate Mendelian genetics. If jumping genes and viral interference were the rule, the germ cells would be a hotchpotch of DNA whose inheritance would be as unpredictable as pangenes. By and large, it is not the rule. Modern Mendelian genetics accounts for orderly predictable inheritance, which is the rule. Mutation – and all the new developments that can be put under that umbrella – puts variety into the system but does not alter the underlying rule.

Breeding programmes of the last eighty years are nonsensical if Mendelian and mutation inheritance is not the explanation of inherited variation. The Soviet belief in the inheritance of acquired characters – and its application to plant breeding – led to an agricultural catastrophe in Russia.

11. Selection in Action

'Can the principle of selection which we have seen is so potent in the hands of man, apply in nature?' Darwin 1859.

The Darwin-Wallace theory was an important advance on all previous evolutionary theories because it provided an acceptable mechanism for evolution. It linked the Malthusian theory of population control with the successful results of animal breeding. Selection from dissimilar individuals was the guiding force of evolution. Selection – either natural or sexual – maintained things as they were or effected change.

But – domestic animals apart – it was difficult to find examples of selection in action. Only the results of selection were evident. Darwin picked the heather-coloured red grouse and the peaty-coloured black grouse to illustrate natural selection. Grouse, he argued, would increase 'in countless numbers' if they did not 'suffer' from birds of prey. The selective agents were the hawk and the colour of the habitat: 'I can see no reason to doubt that natural selection might be most effective in giving the proper colour to each kind of grouse.' So long as grouse differed slightly from one another there would be differential selection for camouflage. 'Less than a grain in the balance,' he wrote in the unpublished 1844 *Essay*, 'will determine which individuals shall live and which perish.' Wallace, too, noticed grouse. The British red grouse, he pointed out, was closely related to the Scandinavian grouse but, unlike its relative, did not become white in winter. During the short time it had been isolated – about 7000 years – the British grouse had evolved an unchanging plumage in response to a comparatively unchanging environment.

Darwin was aware that such examples were hypothetical:

'whether natural selection has really thus acted in nature, in modifying and adapting the various forms of life to their several conditions and stations,' he wrote in the *Origin*, 'must be judged by the general tenour and balance of evidence given in the following chapters.' Most of his examples of selection were drawn – unlike Wallace's – from domestic animals. 'I have found it very important associating with fanciers and breeders,' he told Huxley a few days after the publication of the *Origin*, 'for instance, I sat one evening in a gin palace in the Borough amongst a set of pigeon fanciers' – and – 'recognized how little crossing has had to do with improving breeds.' Thus, he was able – from such information gained from personal contact – to conclude in the *Origin* that man and nature were selecting infinitesimal differences in the production of new breeds and species. Selection 'consists', he wrote, 'in the great effect produced by the accumulation in one direction during successive generations, of differences absolutely inappreciable by an uneducated eye.' Thus had the fantail, the pouter, the tumbler and the grouse evolved.

Critics of the *Origin* were quick to point out that Darwin had in no way proved that natural selection worked. François Pictet granted – he later became converted – that Darwin had explained the probable action of natural selection 'very well' but, he believed, Darwin 'accords it too much importance.' And Adam Sedgwick asked rhetorically: 'as to your grand principle – *natural selection* – what is it but a secondary consequence of your supposed or known, primary facts?' Richard Owen denounced it because it would take too long to effect any evolutionary change.

Natural selection was not easy to observe in action. But towards the end of the nineteenth century – in North America – H. C. Bumpus studied the selective effect of a snowstorm on house sparrows. He found that sparrows that died in the storm differed significantly in weight and wing length from sparrows that survived.

Once the Mendelian genes appeared on the scene, mathematicians got to work on selection. In 1905, Hardy and Weinberg established independently that mutant genes – however deleterious in the homozygous state – would not be quickly eliminated from a population. The gene could be carried – its deleterious effect masked by its partner – in the heterozygote. Darwin's white mouse, though eliminated by selection, would reappear regularly because the white gene was carried in the heterozygous grey mice. Selection, therefore, might act for uniformity in populations but genetic variations – even without new mutations – would not be eliminated. The uniformity would be an average – the uniformity of the majority – but variants would always turn up.

Other mathematical models of evolutionary change were constructed: taking into account population size, the speed of gene spread through populations, mutation rate and selection pressure. Medium-sized populations proved better models for evolutionary change than large populations or small populations. Large populations swamped a favourable gene. Small populations provided too little variability for adaptive evolution and were – as Darwin knew from his island studies – 'greatly retarded' in their evolution and liable to extinction. But small populations more or less isolated from one another were a good model: selection could work differently on each population; occasional intermigration could mix up the genes and provide variability; and adaptation to changing conditions could be rapid. Human populations might have evolved in just such a way. In the nineteenth century, more than 70 per cent of marriages in country districts – in England and Wales – were between men and women living within five miles of each other. But there were always some marriages where the partners had lived a greater distance apart.

But what was a small population? Theoretically, a small population might comprise 100 to 200 individuals, a large population more like 10,000. Many semi-isolated villages in the nineteenth century had 300 to 700 inhabitants. Experimental populations of 10,000 fruitflies have characteristics of large populations. How fast could a 'new' gene spread through such populations?

In the laboratory, a medium-sized population of light and dark fruitflies was kept damp and at an unusually low temperature. The darks did better than the lights and after only ten generations the population was dark. A change in temperature and humidity is easily imaginable in natural conditions but would selection ever be so intense and so rapid in the wild? Calculated selection pressure was of the order of 0.1 per cent for one gene. At that rate, it would take more than 10,000 generations to raise the frequency of a gene from one in a million to one in two. That seemed slow but there had been a lot of geological time for natural selection. In the *Vestiges*, sufficient marginal advantage had been estimated, following Babbage, as one in a hundred million or 0.00001 per cent.

An experimental observation of natural selection in action was made in the 1950s. The black-and-white peppered moth is found all over the British Isles. In 1848, a black variety was recorded from Manchester. By 1895, almost all moths of that species recorded in Manchester were black. It seemed worth investigating. In 1955, a Dorset population of peppered moths with 5.4 per cent of the black variety was compared with a Birmingham population with 89 per cent. Moths were marked and released in both areas. Later, both populations were sampled. The surviving number of black forms and peppered forms was counted. Black forms were being eliminated in Dorset, peppered forms in Birmingham. The selective agents were birds – picking conspicuous individuals off trees – which was confirmed when dead moths were pinned to tree trunks and filmed. Redstarts, hedge sparrows and robins – in the sooty trees of Birmingham – picked forty-three peppered moths for every fifteen black moths off the trees. That was selection at work. The black moths had spread as the polluted trees of the industrial Midlands lost their pale lichens. But the city population did not become 100 per cent black nor did the few blacks disappear from the Dorset population. Was selection incapable of bringing about replacement? Or was selection more complicated than anyone suspected? A moth did not spend its life on a tree trunk. It fluttered about and, according to habitat, flew through shafts of light, shadows or uniform greyness. Even in polluted areas, the sun shone once in a while and put the black moth at a momentary disadvantage. But the pollution was a major selective factor in the spread of the black-wing gene: with the Clean Air Act, the proportion of black moths in the city population dropped.

On spoil heaps of old metal mines in Wales, grasses are rapidly becoming adapted to toxic copper and zinc.

And in the human population individual genes have been selected for disease resistance. The sickle-cell haemoglobin gene can be fatal in a double dose: the unfortunate owner dies of anaemia. But it is a different story when the sickle-cell gene is paired with a normal haemoglobin gene. Then, the owner has a real advantage. In a malaria-ridden country, he is less likely to develop symptoms of malaria than a man who has two normal haemoglobin genes. In most parts of Europe – where there is no malaria – the sickle-cell gene does not exist.

Selection has evolved flies resistant to DDT, rats resistant to warfarin and bacteria resistant to drugs.

Selection occurs – and it can change the proportional representation of a gene in a population much faster than anyone suspected: a hundred times faster, in fact. But one gene does not make a species. Species differ in many genes. And gene build-up to speciation has not been observed.

Darwin believed that one species could turn into another by slow change over long periods of time but he also believed that species diverged from one another: one species became two or more. But although his book was called *On the Origin of Species by Means of Natural Selection*, he said little about the conditions in which species divergence would occur. Species were normally reproductively isolated from each other because, if they were not, the genes would tend to mix and the species would not retain their identity: 'isolation,' Darwin wrote, 'by checking immigration and consequently competition, will give time for any new variety to be slowly proved; and this may sometimes be of importance in the production of new species.' Spatial isolation came to be regarded as an essential prerequisite of species formation.

At the end of the nineteenth century, some naturalists argued that isolation as such would lead to speciation: because gene differences would accumulate randomly and lead to differentiation. Wallace was particularly against that argument because, he replied, it was extremely unlikely that two habitats would be identical and if they were then speciation would not occur because gene differences would not accumulate. But the idea of random accumulation of gene differences regardless of selective value persisted. The accumulation of random gene differences became known as genetic drift. In its extreme form, genetic drift implied – like orthogenesis and neutral genes – that the direction of evolution was determined by the genes and, further, that evolution was non-adaptive. The theory of genetic drift led to many acrimonious debates among biologists largely because, although it was obviously possible in theory, no one knew whether it actually happened. Experimental work on the fruitfly in the USA provided some insight into the possibilities. Genetically similar laboratory populations left unmolested for a certain time varied in relative genetic composition at the end of it. Small populations allowed to increase were more variable than large populations that maintained a steady number. In the final analysis, it seemed that some genes in expanding populations – particularly neutral genes – might increase relatively more than others without any apparent adaptive reason but that, when populations reached a certain size, selection became the overriding determinant of gene proportions. Once again, the Darwin-Wallace theory seemed to triumph.

But what about the sudden appearance of new species in the

fossil record? What about fossil man? What about 300 fruitfly species evolving in Hawaii in only five million years? What about horses? What about the 170 fish species swimming in Lake Victoria? Have they all evolved by differential selection during periods of temporary isolation? Or are they examples of speciation by saltation after all?

Already in 1900 – with de Vriesian mutations – there seemed to be a mechanism for the attractive and persistent theory of jerky evolution without selection. Bateson and Galton were enthusiastic. Wallace was horrified: mutation was a theory 'before which we poor Darwinians must hide our diminished heads.' Even when de Vriesian mutations were replaced by small-scale gene mutations, the idea of saltation persisted.

In the 1940s, a good case was made for explaining small-scale changes and large-scale changes by different mechanisms. Small-scale changes – even speciation – could be the result of gene variation and natural selection. But new genera or families required saltation; and the cause of saltation was major chromosomal changes – additions, fusions, breaks and polyploidy.

There was no doubt that polyploidy occurred; that it occurred suddenly; that it reproductively isolated the new form from the parents; and that it was widespread among plants where it could be maintained by vegetative reproduction. Polyploidy – the multiplication of whole sets of chromosomes – was a confined case of saltation. But could it survive without selection? Polyploid plants – with big cells and slow turnover – might be less vulnerable to the environment. Less vulnerable – than plants with small cells – to the combined effects of poor soil, unpredictable weather and short growing season. It might account for the success of polyploids in northern countries. More chromosomes means more genes and more genes means more variation for selection to work on. Thus, selection could account for polyploid plant survival.

But what about jump speciation in animals? In the social

structure there may be a clue. In populations with a harem system, a simple chromosome change could become established fast. Horses maintain harems. The striking differences in chromosome number in horse species could be accounted for by mating pattern. Suppose two chromosomes joined – end to end – in the stallion: the new chromosome would be inherited by a large number of foals and one – most likely – would be the next dominant male. The new chromosome would increase rapidly in number until homozygous horses with two new chromosomes were common. There would be a subtle advantage in having two new chromosomes instead of only one: one new chromosome – without a new chromosome partner at cell division – upsets the manufacture of germ cells; two new chromosomes, partnered, do not. Horses with two new chromosomes would be more fertile than horses with one. Such a scenario provides a description of rapid speciation but it does not say which – chromosome mutations or selection – is the directing force of evolution.

Other species – like Hawaiian fruitflies – might be similarly accounted for. But, more often than not, they turn out to be examples of conventional neo-Darwinism: Lake Victoria collected water from many river systems in the past; that could account for many of its different fish; other species could have evolved in the broken habitat of the shallows. Sand bars and fallen rocks – as barriers – provide adequate isolation for gene differences to accumulate by selection: adaptation to rock or sand; adaptation to a diet of snails or shrimps.

Ring species provide a good Darwinian example of what, otherwise, might appear to be saltation. Two similar species of gull exist in Britain: the pale herring gull and the lesser black-backed gull. In North America, there are only herring gulls; round the Bering Straits, there are dark herring gulls; further round, inside Siberia, there are pale black-backed gulls. When they meet in Britain they are distinct species but – round the pole – the semi-isolated populations are interconnected. It would be hard to find a better example of 'apparent' saltation: 'we forget',

Darwin wrote in the *Origin*, 'that groups of species may elsewhere have long existed and have slowly multiplied before they invaded the ancient archipelagoes of Europe and of the United States.'

Extinction, for Darwin, provided good evidence of natural selection at work. If the environment changed quickly, a population might be too small – not variable enough – for selection to change it fast enough for the new conditions: 'any form', said Darwin, 'represented by few individuals will, during fluctuations in the seasons or in the number of its enemies, run a good chance of utter extinction.' Small populations of big animals – big animals have long life cycles – would be the ones most likely to become extinct in changed conditions. Spectacular extinctions, like the extinction of the dinosaurs, might have been caused by changes in climate and vegetation combined with evolutionary inertia associated with big animals. Opponents of Darwinism put extinction down to catastrophe: such as comet impacts or racial senility. But extinction can be seen in action. Man drained the reed swamps of North China and Père David's deer was wiped out. He cut down the forest and the Carolina parakeet became extinct. He burnt the undergrowth and the Chatham rail became extinct. He took his cat to an island and wiped out a wren. A comparatively slight change in the environment was sufficient for a sudden extinction.

Adaptation to environment by natural selection – the Darwin-Wallace theory – is nowhere more apparent than in extreme conditions. Environmental adaptation has elicited a similar evolutionary response from widely dissimilar animals and plants. Convergence, as it is called, impressed Darwin on the *Beagle* voyage: 'several species having the same general habitats, occupying analogous situations and obviously filling the same place in the natural economy.' The deserts of Patagonia and Syria – guanacos or gazelles, agoutis or hares – were an example of convergence which, Darwin exclaimed, 'strikes me with wonder'. Desert adaptation offers an extreme example of environmental pressure on animals and plants to conform. Kangaroo rats in America – jumping jerboas in Asia and Africa, marsupial mice in Australia – jumping through the desert night on long legs, fluffy feet, tufted tail at the balance. In Africa, euphorbias; cactuses, in America: both store water in fat green stems. The dark forest selects climbers: climbing by leaves, climbing by roots, climbing by tendrils, twining 'to reach the light and', Darwin wrote, 'to expose a large surface of their leaves to its action and to that of the free air.' The extreme requirements of underground conditions select spade-legged moles, mole-rats and mole-crickets. A diet of termites selects New World anteaters and Old World pangolins: giant claws shatter the nest; long sticky tongues – from toothless snouts – probe and pick out the struggling termites. It struck Darwin 'with wonder' – natural selection at work.

But what about man? How has he evolved? Can natural selection account for the human species or is sexual selection – as Darwin believed – the key to man's evolution?

Darwin's theory of sexual selection had two main components: female choice and male rivalry. Female choice, as an evolutionary mechanism, has had its ups and downs. In courtship displays, colour and adornment can enhance a male's performance, can stimulate a female for coition. Mutant fruitflies can fail to stimulate a female. But does the female 'choose' between one gene constitution and another or does the mutant fail to chase away rivals? Female damsel fish 'choose' aggressive males: male damsel fish guard the fertilized eggs; aggressive males will see off predators. But super-aggressive males – totally preoccupied with seeing off predators – lose the eggs, like unaggressive males. Damsel fish could illustrate sexual selection of 'moderate' aggression by female choice or natural selection for egg survival. Reproductive success is the measure of survival.

The female choice component of sexual selection is less acceptable than Darwin's male rivalry. In North America, 7 per cent of male sage grouse achieve 85 per cent of the matings. The successful males are the oldest males. Is it natural selection for longevity or is it sexual selection by male rivalry? Big deer with big antlers fertilize more hinds and produce more fawns than small deer with small antlers. Animal societies often favour the evolution of aggressive characters associated with male rivalry: giving one male – as opposed to another – the opportunity to transmit his genes to the offspring.

The male rivalry component of sexual selection was the key, Darwin believed, to the evolution of man: 'of all the causes which have led to the differences in external appearance between the races of man, and to a certain extent between man and the lower animals, sexual selection has been the most efficient.'

Male rivalry, Darwin argued, would account for the difference in size between man and woman. Big males and small females occur in other primates, too: baboons, orang utans, gorillas and chimpanzees. A strongly marked difference is associated with harem systems: the dominant male gorilla, twice the weight of the female, holds together his harem of females and juveniles. A less marked male and female size difference is associated with multi-male troops of chimpanzee. No size difference between male and female is found in monogamous gibbons. Male rivalry, associated with success in mating, could account for size difference. There is no evidence of female choice – that other component of sexual selection.

Male rivalry might not be the only factor to account for evolution of male and female size difference. It could be attributed to natural selection and not all the pressure need be on the male. Darwin looked for a single cause. Wallace postulated different selective agencies acting on males and females. Differential selection might favour big males feeding on the ground, small females eating in trees: sharing out meagre food resources. Differential selection might favour the big protective male and the small – quick maturing – female.

Social organization itself could be subject to natural selection.

Food gathering – a selective agent as important as reproduction –
might favour one social organization in one environment, not in
another. The gorilla, predominantly a leaf-eater, lives in
generous conditions but confined to a small area. The male has
no problem keeping his harem together. The gorilla can protect
his females as they feed together on the ground – but there is a
group premium on male size and strength. The chimpanzee
searches a wide area: seeking scattered food sources, seeking the
odd tree in fruit. Males co-operate in the defence of the area and
for this co-operative role selection has favoured males only
marginally bigger than females.

Human size difference approximates more to the
chimpanzee's than to the gorilla's or the monogamous gibbon's.
Early hominids were scavenging omnivores, searching for fruit
and carcasses. Did man and woman, therefore, evolve, like the
chimpanzee, as a promiscuous group? Male and female size
difference squares neatly with that hypothesis but testis size does
not. Man has relatively small testes. In other primates, relatively
small testes are associated with harems and monogamy. The
message, so far, is unclear.

Harem systems and multi-male systems – where dominant
males contribute a disproportionate number of genes to the next
generation – can favour rapid speciation. Man differs from the
chimpanzee and the gorilla in the gross morphology of one
chromosome. One big human chromosome has been derived
from end-to-end fusion of two small ape chromosomes. The
spread of that new chromosome – like those horse chromosomes
– could have been rapid in a social group with dominant males.
Homo, after all, might have jumped into existence from his ape-
like ancestor.

Whatever the social structure, man has been social for a long
time. In human society, division of labour provided evolutionary
advantages. As a social animal, man has evolved his unique
characteristics. Altruism, too, has been of advantage to the
group, as Darwin realized. In the *Origin*, he gave an example of

what the sociobiologists call kin selection. If a bull is slaughtered and declared, after slaughter, to be best quality meat, what can the breeder do? He selects stock from the bull's siblings because they share his qualities. The bird that warns its chicks, though it loses its life, ensures the survival of its genes. The baby-sitting jackal, that minds its brothers and sisters, is minding its own genes and learning to be a parent. Division of labour and altruism – among men and chimpanzees – would have been favoured in groups where members were related.

Gradual adaptation and speciation by natural selection, saltation with selection, saltation without selection – that is still the question for those who, like Darwin, are 'fully convinced that species are not immutable'.

12. A Working Hypothesis

> 'Now this hypothesis may be tested – and this seems to me the only fair and legitimate manner of considering the whole question – by trying whether it explains several large and independent classes of facts,' Darwin 1859.

'How true is the theory of evolution?' asked *Nature* in 1981. The question was answered by a film loop at the British Museum of Natural History in South Kensington: 'the concept of evolution by natural selection is not strictly speaking scientific.' If it is not true, if it is not scientific – then what is truth? And what is science?

Darwin's theory has been criticized for its lack of philosophical stringency. It has been labelled a bad theory because it means everything to everyone. It has been labelled a bad theory because it is not falsifiable. And it has been criticized because it has no predictive value.

A lot of the criticism has come from philosophers.

Comments by Popper some years ago on the unscientific nature of Darwinian theory – that it was not subject to experiment, that it was not falsifiable – have percolated through to the public. Evolution is not falsifiable because it consists of unique and, therefore, unrepeatable events. Evolutionary theory, Popper concluded, was not science but a 'metaphysical research programme'.

That unfortunate description brought the creationists cheering into the Museum. So loud they cheered . . . the echoes reached the Head of Public Services Department. They were granted a placard – at the entrance to the 'Origin of Species' exhibition – that proclaimed in bold letters the creationist view that 'living things' had been 'created perfect and unchanging'. Thus, the Darwinian theory – or evolution by natural selection –

was discredited at the entrance. It was a triumph for the creationists and total bewilderment for the public. 'Darwin's death in South Kensington', announced a leading article in *Nature*.

How does the scientist have an idea? Is it the result of induction or deduction? Does the method make it a good or a bad idea? Philosophers of science, like Sedgwick, had no doubts that only inductive method was acceptable: assemble facts any old how and then develop an hypothesis. The *Origin*, Sedgwick thought, was not the result of inductive method. But Darwin maintained that he had used the Baconian inductive method, conscientiously. But he admitted that, on one occasion, he had the idea before the facts: 'no other work of mine was begun in so deductive a spirit as this, for the whole theory was thought out on the west coast of South America, before I had seen a true coral reef.' But Darwin's notebooks show that he used deductive method frequently.

DARWIN 1876: 'I worked on true Baconian principles, and without any theory collected facts.' (*Autobiography*)

SEDGWICK 1860: 'It [the *Origin*] has deserted the inductive track – the only track that leads to physical truth.' (*Spectator*)

DARWIN 1860: 'On his standard of proof, *natural selection* would never progress, for without the making of theories I am convinced there would be no observation.' (*Letter to C. Lyell*)

HAUGHTON 1860: 'No progress in natural science is possible as long as men will take their rude guesses at truth for facts.' (*Natural History Review*)

DARWIN 1876: 'Here then I had at last got a theory by which to work.' (*Autobiography*)

KANT 1786: 'I assert that whenever a dispute has raged for any length of time, especially in philosophy, there was, at the bottom of it, never a problem about mere words, but always a genuine problem about things.' (*Metaphysical Foundations of Natural Science*)

MACBETH 1971: 'Darwin was an amateur. He did not teach in a university or work in a laboratory.' (*Darwin Retried*)

Anyone can have an idea but the scientist – in order to be scientific – has to support the idea. He has several options. The first and most obvious is to assemble facts. Darwin's work was a staggering array of facts drawn from experience and drawn from extensive reading.

DARWIN 1868: 'I believe in the truth of the theory, because it collects under one point of view, and gives a rational explanation of many apparently independent classes of facts.' (*Variations of Animals and Plants under Domestication*)

MIVART 1871: 'Although the style of the work is, as we have said, fascinating, nevertheless we think that the author is somewhat encumbered with the multitude of his facts, which at times he seems hardly able to group and handle so effectively as might be expected from his special talent.' (*Quarterly Review*)

DARWIN 1881: 'My industry has been nearly as great as it could have been in the observation and collection of facts. I have had the strongest desire to understand or explain whatever I observed – that is, to group all facts under some general laws.' (*Autobiography*)

ELIOT 1859: 'Sadly wanting in illustrative facts.' (*Adam Bede*)

But a collection of facts to be valuable must not only corroborate the idea but shape the idea into an hypothesis. But the hypothesis must be a simple hypothesis. Science must follow the 'law of parsimony' invented in the fourteenth century by a Franciscan, William of Ockham: 'entities are not to be multiplied beyond necessity.'

141

SPENCER 1860: 'That which alone can unify knowledge must be the law of co-operation of all the factors – a law expressing simultaneously the complex antecedents and the complex consequents which any phenomenon as a whole presents.' (*Westminster Review*)

PATTERSON 1978: 'The modern theory of evolution is the basis of biological science. It is an idea that unifies and directs work in all sorts of specialized fields, from medicine to geology.' (*Evolution*)

POPPER 1935: 'A high degree of simplicity is nevertheless linked with a high degree of corroboration.' (*The Logic of Scientific Discovery*)

MAYR 1963: 'The theory of evolution is quite rightly called the greatest unifying theory in biology.' (*Animal Species and Evolution*)

A method that can be used to test the scientific idea – or hypothesis – is argument by analogy. Darwin's idea which 'explained' unique historical events, replacing the idea of essences with the idea of change, could be tested for credibility. Following Herschel, Darwin used argument by analogy: natural selection – by analogy with selective breeding of domestic animals – was credible.

HERSCHEL 1831: 'If the analogy of two phenomena is very close and striking, while, at the same time, the cause of one is very obvious, it becomes scarcely possible to refuse to admit the action of an analogous cause in the other.' (*Preliminary Discourse on the Study of Natural Philosophy*)

WHEWELL 1839: 'If we cannot reason from the analogies of the existing to the events of the past world, we have no foundations for science.' (*Presidential address to the Geological Society*)

POPPER 1980: 'It appears as if some people would think the

historical sciences are untestable because they describe unique events. However, the description of unique events can very often be tested by deriving from them testable predictions.' (*New Scientist*)

DARWIN 1859: 'Analogy would lead me one step further, namely, to the belief that all animals and plants have descended from some one prototype. But analogy may be a deceitful guide.' (*Origin of Species*)

If the assembled facts have supported the idea more often than not – and if sound analogies have been found to explain the unique events – the idea becomes a working hypothesis. Then, the scientist must test the hypothesis by experiment and the experiment must be repeatable. Further experiments must corroborate previous experiments (as de Vries corroborated Mendel). Field studies and laboratory studies have tested by experiment that environment selects variants and stabilizes them in a population. Individual genetic variations within a population have been located and measured: for example, fruitfly, mouse and snail populations. The recolonization of a depopulated island has been monitored. Rocks and fossils have been dated by radioactive assay – though the creationists deny it.

DARWIN 1876: 'An unverified hypothesis is of little or no value; but if any one should hereafter be led to make observations by which some such hypothesis could be established, I have done good service.' (*Autobiography*)

SEDGWICK 1859: 'Many of your conclusions are based on assumptions which can neither be proved nor disproved.' (*Letter to C. Darwin*)

HOPKINS 1860: 'The great defect of this theory is the want of all positive proof.' (*Fraser's Magazine*)

MILL 1875: 'Mr Darwin has never pretended his theory was proved.' (*System of Logic, eighth edition*)

MIVART 1871: 'Mr Darwin's conclusions may be correct but we feel we have now indeed a right to demand that they shall be proved before we assent to them.' (*Quarterly Review*)

POPPER 1935: 'I think we must get accustomed to the idea that . . . science . . . is a system of guesses or anticipations which in principle cannot be justified, but with which we work as long as they stand up to tests.' (*The Logic of Scientific Discovery*)

SHEPPARD 1958: 'Genetical and ecological investigations, coupled with field studies, have revealed many of the agents which control adaptation and speciation.' (*Natural Selection and Heredity*)

PATTERSON 1978: 'Since Darwin's work, the lapse of time has been sufficient for many examples of natural selection to have been observed in nature and in laboratory experiments.' (*Evolution*)

POPPER 1978: 'I have changed my mind about the testability and the logical status of the theory of natural selection; and I am glad to have an opportunity to make a recantation.' (*Dialectics*)

The criterion of falsifiability has methodological value. The scientific idea – or scientific theory – must be exposed to falsification in order to establish its truth. That which does not occur cannot be negated. Darwin devoted a chapter of the first edition of the *Origin* to 'difficulties on theory'. By the sixth edition, there was an additional chapter on 'miscellaneous objections to the theory of natural selection'. Darwin exposed his theory to falsification.

DARWIN 1859: 'For I am well aware that scarcely a single point is discussed in the volume on which facts cannot be adduced, often apparently leading to conclusions directly opposite to those at which I have arrived.' (*Origin of Species*)

SEDGWICK 1860: 'There is a light by which man may see and

comprehend facts and truths such as these. But Darwin wilfully shuts it out from our senses.' (*Spectator*)

DARWIN 1859: 'If it could be demonstrated that any complex organ existed which could not possibly have been formed by numerous, successive slight modifications, my theory would absolutely break down.' (*Origin of Species*)

POPPER 1935: 'It must be possible for an empirical scientific system to be refuted by experience.' (*The Logic of Scientific Discovery*)

DIRECTOR OF THE CREATION-RESEARCH CENTER 1980: 'Negative evidence against evolution is the same as positive evidence for creation.' (*The Sciences*)

Darwin's theory was a gradualist theory but he was aware of sudden appearance of species in the rocks. He was aware of gaps in the fossil record: due to the imperfection of the geological record or due, he conceded, to a real event, a 'missing link'. It could be sudden migration or – when compressed into the crude time scale of the rocks – rapid speciation by natural selection. He did not regard sudden events as evidence against gradualist theory. There are, however, geologists who repudiate Darwinian theory because of the gaps in the fossil record. The creationists have jumped joyfully into the gaps.

HERSCHEL 1863: 'The idea of *jumps* . . . as if for instance a wolf should at some epoch of lupine history take to occasionally littering a dog or a fox among her cubs [would introduce] mind, plan, design.' (*Letter to C. Lyell*)

DARWIN 1861: 'I am not shaken about "*saltus*", I did not write without going pretty carefully into all the cases of normal structure in animals resembling monstrosities which appear *per saltus*.' (*Letter to J. Hooker*)

BRONN 1860: 'We need no longer doubt as before in the possibility of later discoveries gradually filling in the enormous gaps which now confront us . . . However, as long as this is not possible, Darwin's theory is as impossible as ever.' (*Neues Jahrbuch für Mineralogie*)

FAWCETT 1860: 'It might appear according to the geological record that whole groups of allied species have suddenly come upon the earth.' (*Macmillan's Magazine*)

J. S. HUXLEY 1957: 'With the length of time available, little adjustments can easily be made to add up to miraculous adaptations.' (*New Bottles for New Wine*)

GOULD 1977: 'The reconciliation of our gradualistic ideas with the appearance of discontinuity is a classical problem of intellectual history.' (*Ontogeny and Phylogeny*)

AGASSIZ 1874: 'But little is said of the sudden apparition of powerful original qualities which almost always rise like pure creations and are gone with their day and generation.' (*Atlantic Monthly*)

DARWIN 1868: 'We have no evidence of the appearance, or at least of the continued procreation, under nature of abrupt modifications of structure.' (*Variation in Animals and Plants under Domestication*)

Darwin pointed out that fossils from two consecutive strata were more alike than fossils from two separated strata; that species once extinct were never found in later strata. But if species stopped in one stratum and started again – from scratch – in another, it could be argued that the geological record falsified evolution and supported catastrophism and creation. If the fossil sequence went into reverse, that could falsify evolutionary theory. If two identical organisms had different ancestors, that could cast doubt on the theory, too. Darwin believed firmly in the law that 'nature never repeats herself'.

AGASSIZ 1874: 'This certainly does not look like a connected series beginning with the lowest and ending with the highest,

for the highest fishes come first and the lowest come last.'
(*Atlantic Monthly*)

HUXLEY 1863: 'It is enough that such a view [gradualism] of the
relations of extinct to living beings has been propounded, to
lead us to inquire, with anxiety, how far the recent discoveries
of human remains in a fossil state bear out, or oppose, that
view.' (*Man's Place in Nature*)

DARWIN 1859: 'All the chief laws of palaeontology plainly
proclaim, as it seems to me, that species have been produced
by ordinary generation.' (*Origin of Species*)

CARPENTER 1860: 'To our minds the great wonder is, that
palaeontological research should have already yielded so much
information as to the past life of the globe, not that it should
afford so little.' (*National Review*)

A scientific theory has predictive power. Darwin's theory of coral
reef formation does not predict that all volcanic islands will
become atolls. But the theory of natural selection predicts the
extinction of the giant panda: when its bamboo dies, it dies.
Arguing by analogy, the theory can predict the evolution of
insects resistant to insecticides, plants resistant to toxic wastes.
Probability theory adds a further dimension: the probability of a
mutation can be predicted. Mathematical models are subject to
experiment: models of island colonization, inter-species
competition and evolutionary relationships.

DARWIN 1837: 'These speculations, even if partly true they are
of the greatest service towards the end of science, namely
prediction; till facts are grouped and called there can be no
prediction. The only advantage of discovering laws is to
foretell what will happen and to see bearing of scattered facts.'
(*Species Notebook*)

ELDREDGE & CRACRAFT 1980: 'This prediction is based on our
expectation that the evolutionary process that produced a

single unique history of life, and that changes in organisms and their features will conform to the pattern of this history more often than not.' (*Phylogenetic Patterns and the Evolutionary Process*)

OLDROYD 1980: 'We can hardly suppose that the Darwinian theory will tell us with similar precision which species are going to survive in the future; which will become extinct.' (*Darwinian Impacts*)

REICHENBACH 1930: 'We should say that it serves to decide upon probability. For it is not given to science to reach either truth or falsity . . . but scientific statements can only attain continuous degrees of probability.' (*Erkenntnis*)

After 123 years, Darwinism is still a controversial issue. Much of the controversy is philosophical and semantic. Darwinism is dead. Or is it? What is Darwinism? Is it confined to the *Origin*? To *Variation*? To *The Descent of Man*? Today, pangenesis has been replaced by Mendelism. Saltation is possible and sexual selection has a new look. But Darwinism is still the theory of evolution by means of natural selection. Whether Darwinism is a good theory or a bad theory – whether it is true – is not important. What is important to biologists is that Darwinism is a useful theory – a good working hypothesis – that incorporates the facts 'ready to take their proper places as soon as the theory which would receive them was sufficiently explained'.

NATURE 1981: 'One of the remarkable features of the theory is that it remains consistent with the vastly greater body of data now available.' (*Editorial*)

FAWCETT 1860: 'If Mr Darwin's theory were disproved tomorrow, the volume in which it is expounded would still remain one of our most interesting, most valuable, and most accurate treatises on natural history.' (*Macmillan's Magazine*)

MILL 1874: 'He has opened a path of inquiry full of promise, the results of which none can foresee. And is it not a wonderful feat of scientific knowledge and ingenuity to have rendered so bold a suggestion, which the first impulse of every one was to reject at once, admissible and discussable, even as a conjecture?' (*System of Logic, eighth edition*)

CAPLAN 1981: 'The point is that evolutionary theory, like all theories in science is constantly tested, refined, modified, adapted and rewritten.' (*Nature*)

Only those who do not accept adaptation by natural selection – who believe in non-adaptive evolution or creation – are anti-Darwin. Non-adaptive evolution can be tested. Creation cannot be tested by any observable phenomena or scientific experiment. Creation cannot be shown to be true or false. It is not a scientific theory like Darwinism.

DARWIN 1859: 'It is so easy to hide our ignorance under such expressions as the "plan of creation", "unity of design", etc, and to think that we give an explanation.' (*Origin of Species*)

PALEY 1819: 'There cannot be design without a designer, contrivance without a contriver.' (*Natural Theology*)

HUXLEY 1886: 'What, therefore, is his authority on the matter: creation by Deity – which cannot be tested.' (*Scientific Memoirs*)

MACKIE 1981: 'Creation science is a myth which depends on a dogmatic and deductive faith in the existence of God who has intervened frequently on Earth to make new living things out of nothing and, this being so, the Natural History Museum may be said to have betrayed both its scientific status and its educational role by implying that this myth is somehow on the same intellectual plane as the theory of evolution.' (*Nature*)

The theory has become adapted by the forces of selection: it has evolved – it has crept insidiously into everyday use. 'New ideas, if good and true,' said Wallace, 'become adapted and utilized, while if untrue, or if not adequately presented to the world, they are rejected or forgotten.'

That the Darwin-Wallace theory will survive the next hundred years is 'only a hypothesis'. But Huxley has the last word on Darwinism.

'Do not allow yourselves to be misled by the common notion that an hypothesis is untrustworthy simply because it is an hypothesis.'

Biographical Chronology

1809	Charles Robert Darwin born 12 February at Shrewsbury in England, fifth child of Robert Waring Darwin and Susannah Wedgwood.
1817–18	Day school in Shrewsbury.
1818–25	Dr Butler's boarding school in Shrewsbury.
1825–7	Edinburgh University Medical School.
1828–31	Christ's College Cambridge ordinary arts degree course.
1831–6	On voyage of the *Beagle*.
1837	Starts species notebooks.
1838	Starts man notebooks.
1839	Marries his cousin Emma Wedgwood and lives at Upper Gower Street in London.
	Journal and Remarks: vol. 3 of *Narrative of the Surveying Voyage of HMS 'Beagle'*.
	Starts on fertilization of flowers.
1842	*The Structure and Distribution of Coral Reefs.*
	Pencil *Sketch* of 'my species theory'.
	Moves to Down in Kent.
1844	*Geological Observations on the Volcanic Islands Visited during the Voyage of HMS 'Beagle'.*
	Essay on species theory.
1846	*Geological Observations on South America.*
	Starts on barnacles.
1851	*A Monograph of the Sub-Class Cirripedia with Figures of all the Species. The Lepadidae; or Pedunculated Cirripedes.*

> *A Monograph of the Fossil Lepadidae; or Pedunculated Cirripedes of Great Britain.*

1853   Royal Medal of the Royal Society.

1854   *The Balanidae (or Sessile Cirripedes); the Verrucidae etc.*

> *A Monograph of the Fossil Balanidae and Verrucidae of Great Britain.*

> Sorts notes for *Natural Selection* (provisional title).

1858   The 'bolt from the blue': Wallace's article from the Moluccas.

> Darwin-Wallace theory announced at the Linnean Society.

1859   *On the Origin of Species by Means of Natural Selection, or the Preservation of Favoured Races in the Struggle for Life.*

1860   Starts on *Variation*.

> Starts on insectivorous plants.

1861   Starts on orchids.

1862   *The Various Contrivances by which Orchids are Fertilised by Insects.*

1863   Starts on climbing plants.

1864   Copley Medal of the Royal Society.

1868   *The Variation of Animals and Plants under Domestication.*

1871   *The Descent of Man, and Selection in Relation to Sex.*

1872   *The Expression of the Emotions in Man and Animals.*

1875   *The Movements and Habits of Climbing Plants.*

> *Insectivorous Plants.*

1876   *The Effects of Cross and Self Fertilisation in the Vegetable Kingdom.*

1877   *The Different Forms of Flowers on Plants of the Same Species.*

> Starts on movement of plants.

> LL.D. Cambridge.

1880   *The Power of Movement in Plants.*

1881   *The Formation of Vegetable Mould, through the Action of Worms, with Observations on their Habits.*

1882   Dies 19 April at Down.
        Buried 26 April in Westminster Abbey.

Glossary

'This glossary, which has been given because several readers have complained to me that some of the terms used were unintelligible to them,' Darwin 1872.

ALBINO: without pigment.

ALBUMEN: white of egg.

ANTHER: that part of the stamen that produces pollen.

ATOLL: coral reef surrounding a central shallow lagoon.

BARRIER REEF: coral reef along an island or mainland shore separated by a lagoon.

BRECCIA: deposit of angular fragments of rock.

CATASTROPHE: fire, earthquake, flood.

CHROMOSOME: one of a set of nuclear units characteristic of a species, consisting of genes; e.g. man has forty-six chromosomes, chimpanzee forty-eight.

CIRCUMNUTATION: for Darwin, elliptical or spiral movement of a growing shoot or tendril.

CIRRUS: of barnacles, thoracic appendage.

CLADISTIC CLASSIFICATION: non-evolutionary classification of animals and plants by specialized characters.

CLADOGRAM: non-evolutionary branching-tree diagrams where group relationships are displayed at the tips of the branches.

CLASS: groups of related orders; e.g. Mammalia.

CONTINENTAL ISLAND: island that was once part of a continent.

COTYLEDON: first leaf of a plant.

CYTOLOGY: science of cells.

DIMORPHISM: two distinct forms; e.g. male and female.

DIPLOID: having a set of chromosomes derived half from the female and half from the male parent. Most organisms are diploid

DNA: deoxyribonucleic acid: molecule that codes for hereditary characteristics, the double helix.

DIOECY: separate sexes: male flowers on one plant, female flowers on another

DOMINANT: the prevailing gene of a pair.

EMBRYOLOGY: science of development from egg to adult.

ENTROPY: disorganized energy.

ENZYME: protein catalyst which speeds a chemical reaction in the body such as oxidation.

FAMILY: group of related genera; e.g. Hominidae.

FAULT: fracture in the earth's crust on either side of which there has been relative movement.

FRENUM: fold of skin.

FRINGING REEF: coral reef along an island or mainland shore not separated by a lagoon.

GEMMULE: for Darwin, a minute particle carrying information from body cells to germ cells and contributing to the hereditary make-up of the next generation: a pangene.

GENE: unit of heredity: a length of DNA.

GENUS: group of related species; e.g. *Homo*.

GEOTROPISM: responding by movement to the stimulus of gravity.

GERM CELL: reproductive cell.

HAEMOGLOBIN: red respiratory blood pigment.

HAPLOID: having half the normal set of chromosomes; e.g. germ cells are haploid.

HELIOTROPISM: responding by movement to the stimulus of light.

HERMAPHRODITE: individual with both male and female reproductive organs.

HETEROSTYLY: of plants, having unlike styles.

HETEROZYGOTE: having paired unlike genes.

HIPPOCAMPUS MINOR: thickened part of the floor of the cerebral cortex associated with memory.

HOMOLOGY: similarity of structure due to common ancestry but not necessarily with similar function.

HOMOZYGOTE: having paired like genes.

HYBRID: cross-bred animal or plant; or heterozygote.

IGNEOUS ROCK: rock formed directly from molten silicate melt: volcanic rock.

INTERMAXILLARY: between the upper jaw bones.

INVERTEBRATE: animal without a backbone.

LARVA: free-living embryo, usually distinctly different from the adult.

MISSING LINK: gap in the fossil record.

MORPHOLOGY: science of form and structure.

MUTATION: heritable alteration in a gene or chromosome.

NECTARY: group of cells in a flower secreting sweet substance.

NUCLEIC ACID: DNA or RNA.

NUCLEUS: that part of the cell that contains the chromosomes.

NUMERICAL CLASSIFICATION: *see* phenetic classification.

OCEANIC ISLAND: island that was never part of a continent.

ORDER: group of related families; e.g. Primates.

OVIGEROUS: egg-bearing.

OVUM: female germ cell.

PALAEONTOLOGY: science of fossil plants and animals.

PANGENE: *see* gemmule.

PARTHENOGENESIS: reproduction by means of an un-fertilized egg.

PEDUNCLE: flower stalk.

PELORIC: regular flower-shape where irregular is the norm.

PHENETIC CLASSIFICATION: non-evolutionary classifi-cation of animals and plants by number of characters.

PHYLOGENY: evolutionary relationship.

PHYLUM: group of related classes; e.g. Chordata.

PIN-EYED FLOWER: having a long style.

PISTIL: female organ of flower: ovary, style and stigma.

POLLEN: powder containing the pollen grains or male germ cells produced by anthers.

POLYDACTYLY: more than the normal number of fingers or toes.

POLYMORPHISM: many distinct forms in the same population.

POLYPEPTIDE: chain of amino acids out of which proteins are made.

POLYPLOIDY: having more than two sets of chromosomes.

PROBOSCIS: trunk-like process of the head.

PROTEIN: molecule of chains of amino acids; e.g. haemoglobin.

RADIOACTIVE DECAY: alteration effected by a change in the number of charged particles.

RECESSIVE: the subordinate gene of a pair.

RECOMBINATION: genetic combination that results from sexual reproduction.

RETROVIRUS: RNA virus that can code for DNA.

RNA: ribonucleic acid: the molecules that translate the hereditary code into proteins.

ROSTELLUM: of insects, tubular mouthparts.

RUDIMENTARY: of an organ, reduced and useless for its apparent function.

SALTATION: jumping: abrupt variation.

SEDIMENTARY ROCK: formed by deposition in layers of rock fragments and organic remains.

SEGREGATION: unpairing of the genes into separate germ cells.

SOMATIC CELL: body cell as distinct from germ cell.

SPECIES: group of interbreeding individuals not interbreeding with any other group; e.g. *Homo sapiens, Homo erectus.*

SPERMATOZOON: male germ cell.

STAMEN: male organ of a flower: filament and anther.

STIGMA: tip of the pistil that receives pollen.

STYLE: stalk of the pistil supporting the stigma.

TAXON: of classification, any group of plants or animals.
THRUM-EYED FLOWER: having a short style.
VARIETY: individual or group differing slightly from other
   members of the species.
VERTEBRATE: animal with a backbone.

Geological Time Scale
(millions of years ago)

CENOZOIC

holocene	0	– ·01	
pleistocene	·01	– 1·6	
pliocene	1·6	– 7	first human fossils
miocene	7	– 26	
oligocene	26	– 38	
eocene	38	– 54	
palaeocene	54	– 65	

MESOZOIC

cretaceous	65	– 140	
jurassic	140	– 210	first bird fossils
triassic	210	– 245	first mammal fossils

PALAEOZOIC

permian	245	– 290	
carboniferous	290	– 365	first reptile fossils
devonian	365	– 413	first amphibian fossils
silurian	413	– 441	
ordovician	441	– 504	first vertebrate fossils
cambrian	504	– 570	

Further Reading

Allan, M., 1977: *Darwin and his Flowers*, Faber & Faber, London.

Bibby, C., 1959: *T. H. Huxley: Scientist Humanist and Educator*, Watts, London.

Campbell, B., 1972: *Sexual Selection and the Descent of Man*, Heinemann, London.

Darwin, F., 1887: *Life and Letters of Charles Darwin*, Murray, London.

Darwin, F., 1903: *More Letters of Charles Darwin*, Murray, London.

De Beer, G., 1963: *Charles Darwin: Evolution by Natural Selection*, Nelson, London.

Dobzhansky, T., Ayala, F. J., Stebbins, G. L. & Valentine, J. W., 1977: *Evolution*, W. H. Freeman, New York.

Ellegard, A., 1958: *Darwin and the General Reader*, Göteborgs Universitets Arsskrift, Göteborg.

George, W., 1964: *Biologist Philosopher: a Study of the Life and Writing of Alfred Russel Wallace*, Abelard-Schuman, London.

George, W., 1975: *Gregor Mendel and Heredity*, Priory Press, London.

Ghiselin, M. T., 1969: *The Triumph of the Darwinian Method*, University of California Press, Berkeley.

Gillespie, N. C., 1979: *Charles Darwin and the Problem of Creation*, Chicago University Press, Chicago.

Gould, S. J., 1978: *Ever Since Darwin*, Burnett Books, London.

Gruber, H. E., 1974: *Darwin on Man*, Wildwood House, London.

Himmelfarb, G., 1959: *Darwin and the Darwinian Revolution*, Doubleday, New York.

Hull, D. L., 1974: *Philosophy of Biological Science*, Prentice-Hall, Englewood Cliffs, NJ.

Irvine, W., 1955: *Apes, Angels and Victorians*, Weidenfeld & Nicolson, London.

Lyell, K. (ed), 1881: *Life, Letters and Journals of Sir Charles Lyell, Bart*, Murray, London.

Mayr, E., 1963: *Animal Species and Evolution*, Belknap Press, Harvard, Cambridge, Mass.

Morrell, J., and Thackray, A., 1981: *Gentlemen of Science: Early Years of the British Association for the Advancement of Science*, Oxford University Press.

Ruse, M., 1979: *The Darwinian Revolution*, University of Chicago Press, Chicago.

Simpson, G. G., 1949: *The Meaning of Evolution*, Yale University Press, New Haven.

Turrill, W. B., 1963: *Joseph Dalton Hooker*, Nelson, London.

Vorzimmer, P. J., 1972: *Charles Darwin: the Years of Controversy*, English Universities Press, London.

Wilson, L., 1972: *Charles Lyell, the Years to 1841*, Yale University Press, New Haven.